9/06

☆ INSIGHT COMPACT GUIDE

TAHITI

& FRENCH POLYNESIA

Compact Guide: Tahiti is the ultimate quick-reference guide to this exotic South Pacific destination. It tells you everything you'll need to know about Tahiti's Society Islands, from Papeete on Tahiti and Cook's Bay on Moorea to beautiful Bora Bora and magical Huahine, as well as the distant Tuamotu Archipelago. The best beaches, lagoons and resorts are reviewed.

This is one of 130 Compact Guides, combining the interests and enthusiasms of two of the world's best-known information providers: Insight Guides, whose innovative titles have set the standard for visual travel guides since 1970, and Discovery Channel, the world's premier source of non-fiction television programming.

DISCOVERY CHANNEL

APA PUBLICATIONS   L
Part of the Langenscheidt Publishing Group

Insight Compact Guide: Tahiti & French Polynesia

Written by: Nicholas Cobb
Photography by: Tim McKenna
Additional photography by: Philippe Bacchet
Cover picture by: Tim McKenna
Design: Roger Williams
Picture Editor: Hilary Genin
Cartographic Editor: Maria Randell
Maps: Dave Priestley
Design concept: Carlotta Junger

Editorial Director: Brian Bell
Managing Editor: Francis Dorai

CONTACTING THE EDITORS: As every effort is made to provide accurate information in this publication, we would appreciate it if readers would call our attention to any errors and omissions by contacting:
Apa Publications, PO Box 7910, London SE1 1WE, England.
Fax: (44 20) 7403 0290
e-mail: insight@apaguide.co.uk

Information has been obtained from sources believed to be reliable, but its accuracy and completeness, and the opinions based thereon, are not guaranteed.

© 2005 APA Publications GmbH & Co. Verlag KG Singapore Branch, Singapore.

First Edition 2002
Updated 2004 (Reprinted 2005)
Printed in Singapore by Insight Print Services (Pte) Ltd
Original edition © Polyglott-Verlag Dr Bolte KG, Munich

Distributed in the UK & Ireland by:
GeoCenter International Ltd
The Viables Centre, Harrow Way, Basingstoke,
Hampshire RG22 4BJ
Tel: (44 1256) 817 987, Fax: (44 1256) 817 988

Distributed in the United States by:
Langenscheidt Publishers, Inc.
36–36 33rd Street 4th Floor, Long Island City, NY 11106
Tel: (1 718) 784 0055, Fax: (1 718) 784 0640

Worldwide distribution enquiries:
APA Publications GmbH & Co. Verlag KG (Singapore Branch)
38 Joo Koon Road, Singapore 628990
Tel: (65) 6865 1600, Fax: (65) 6861 6438

919.6211
TAH
2005

TaHITI
& FRENCH POLYNESIa

Introduction

Places

Culture

Travel Tips

△ **Watersports (p114)**
Snorkelling in gin-clear waters is one of the many watersports you can do here.

△ **Hotel Bora Bora (p85)**
If you can afford it, this Amanresort is a great place to stay. Pictured here are its over-water bungalows – the ultimate accommodation.

◁ **Musée Gauguin (p44)**
No other artist captures the essence of Tahiti better than Paul Gauguin. His life story is documented at this interesting mueseum at PK 51.2, in the south of Tahiti.

△ **Stone Tiki (p17)**
Tahitians gods are said to inhabit *tiki,* figurines made of stone or wood.

▷ **Flora (p22)**
The yellow and white *Tiare Tahiti* flower. You see these pretty blooms at every turn

◁ **Cook's Bay (p62)**
Moorea's Cook's Bay is the floor of an ancient volcanic crater with spectacular views from its surrounding ridges.

▷ **Cascades de Faarumai (p37)** These spectacular waterfalls, at PK 22 on the east coast of Tahiti, tumble into a crisp, clear pool.

▽ **Rangiroa (p92)**
Ths island's famous Blue Lagoon encloses a smaller lagoon within a larger one.

◁ **Marae Sites (p71)**
Ruins of *marae* — open-air places of worship built to honour the gods — at the village of Maeva. Rituals and sacrifices (sometimes human) were carried out to appease the gods.

▷ **Papeete (p57)**
This busy capital and port town on Tahiti can easily be explored on foot. Pictured here is the Evangelist church by the waterfront.

World's Most Beautiful Islands

Every tropical tourist destination likes to call itself 'paradise on earth,' but in Tahiti and French Polynesia those words have more than a ring of truth. In this sprawling French-accented outpost are jagged green mountains, clear blue lagoons, palm-draped beaches and friendly Polynesians, which together have come to symbolise an earthly heaven.

The novelist James A. Michener described one of its islands, Bora Bora, as the most beautiful in the world. Indeed, Bora Bora's trademark tombstone-like mountain and deep blue lagoon are among the most photographed scenes in the world. Also dramatically beautiful is Moorea, with its tooth-like spires sitting on the rim of an extinct volcano high above two magnificent bays. If postcards could come to life, it would be here on these islands.

The mountains and lagoons form a gorgeous stage for active pursuits ranging from snorkelling and scuba diving to lounging on a pristine beach. You can swim with dolphins, watch sharks in a feeding frenzy a few metres away, or paddle an outrigger canoe to a *motu*, a small islet on the barrier reef. You can walk on well-trodden paths or ride four-wheel-drive vehicles high into the cool mountains. And at night, you can dine on fresh fish from the sea and watch the Tahitians perform the same suggestive dances that helped inspire the famous mutiny on HMS *Bounty* in 1789.

Tahiti and her neighbouring islands are to this day one of the world's most romantic destinations. The tourism industry has augmented the Polynesians' traditionally relaxed way of life with charming guest bungalows built over the coral reefs. Families may not find this a paradise on earth, but couples in love will surely do.

CONTRASTING CULTURES

French Polynesia is both French and Polynesian, a fascinating blend of *haute couture* from Paris and the charming languid ambience of the islands. You are as likely to be met with a '*bonjour*' as with '*ia orana*', the traditional Tahitian greeting.

An earthly paradise
'In the South Seas', wrote the English poet Rupert Brooke in 1914, 'the Creator seems to have laid himself out to show what He can do'.

Left: outrigger canoe, Bora Bora
Below: Sunday best, Papeete
Bottom: bright bougainvillea

Below: French cuisine
Bottom: stringing garlands

The French have brought not just fine wine and excellent cuisine, they have poured billions of francs into the islands. From schools and roads to telecommunications, they have built an infrastructure nearly on a par with Europe and far superior to those on neighbouring South Pacific islands.

Nowhere is the French side of the equation more apparent than in Papeete, on the island of Tahiti. Once a sleepy South Seas port, the capital city is now a busy little metropolis.

But behind the glitzy facade of chic shops lining Boulevard Pomare, the city's busy waterfront promenade, are many reminders of the old Polynesian way of life. This is even more apparent in the rural areas and on the outer islands, where metropolitan ways have had far less impact. Tin roofs may have replaced thatch, and miniskirts taken over grass skirts, but the Tahitians have retained much of their old lifestyles, which adds to the charm of these already beautiful islands.

LOCATION AND LANDSCAPE

French Polynesia lies in the South Pacific Ocean 4,500km (2,800 miles) south of Hawaii and about halfway between North America and Australia. The territory covers a sea area about the size of Europe, yet its 130 main islands only make up some 2,400 sq km (1,500 sq miles) of dry land.

The islands are actually the tops of extinct volcanoes, which rise like stovepipes from the floor of the Pacific Ocean. They were formed millions of years ago when lava escaped from several 'hot spots' as the Pacific Plate slowly moved northwestwards.

Some islands consist of mountains rising high enough to condense moisture from the air into rainfall. In the case of atolls, the mountains have subsided back into sea over the centuries, leaving a chain of narrow islets enclosing a broad lagoon. Other islands like Bora Bora are midway through the geological process: they have both mountainous central islands and rings of islets called *motu* on the barrier reef.

THE ISLAND GROUPS

French Polynesia consists of five island groups, of which the Society Islands – Tahiti, Moorea, Huahine, Raiatea, Tahaa and Bora Bora – are all lush volcanic mountains skirted by narrow coastal plains and surrounded by lagoons enclosed by barrier reefs.

The Society Islands are divided by the direction of the prevailing southeast trade wind, with Tahiti and nearby Moorea known as the Windward Islands because they are upwind of the Leeward Islands – which comprise Huahine, Raiatea, Tahaa and Bora Bora.

To the northeast lies a great chain of atolls known as the Tuamotu Islands, which seafarers have long called the 'Dangerous Archipelago' because they are so low as to be almost impossible to see from a distance at sea level. Most visited of these are Rangiroa, Manihi and Tikehau.

Farther afield are the Marquesas, Austral and Gambier island groups. Only the Marquesas Islands are regularly visited, primarily by passengers on the *Aranui* cruise ship *(see page 116).*

CLIMATE AND WHEN TO GO

The tropical climate is sunny, warm and humid all year round. Recent changes to the world's weather patterns have affected the islands, but in general,

Pack a brolly
Although the traditional wet season is from November to March, tropical showers can dump a few inches of rain on the islands even in the drier winter months from June to August. The handiest and by far the most useful rain gear is a small, folding umbrella which can be tucked away in your shoulder bag.

Below: jagged mountain peak, Tahiti Iti
Bottom: Mt Otemanu, Bora Bora

CLIMATE CHART

Papeete

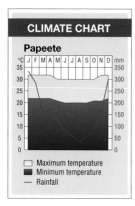

☐ Maximum temperature
■ Minimum temperature
— Rainfall

Traditional outrigger canoe

November through March still is the hotter and more humid summer season, with periods of rain and average daily maximum temperatures of 30°C (86°F), and average lows of 22°C (72°F). The prevailing southeast tradewinds provide nature's air-conditioning during the relatively dry season from June through August. Midday high temperatures average 28°C (82°F), with lows of 20°C (68°F) during this austral winter.

Winter coincides with both the traditional French holiday period and the month-long Heiva i Tahiti festival, the territory's biggest annual event *(see page 104)*. This is the best time of the year to visit, but advance bookings of hotel rooms and airline seats are absolutely essential. Next best are April, May, September and October, when the weather is drier and temperatures lower than during the summer months.

Hotel rates are lowest from November through February, but you run the risk of tropical depressions bringing several days of rain at a time. In addition, there is always a chance of a tropical cyclone striking during these months.

TROPICAL CYCLONES

Originating in the Pacific Ocean between Samoa and southeast French Polynesia, powerful cyclones with wind speeds of up to 120 knots can churn up waves as high as 15m (49 ft). Between 1997 and 1998, hurricanes whipped up by the El Niño phenomena caused extensive destruction in Maupiti and Bora Bora. It is important to note, however, that the threat of cyclones is negligible. Tahiti only gets hit every 5–7 years when El Niño-like warming comes along and disrupts normal weather patterns. Even when the islands are hit by cyclones, these only last a day or two.

THE FIRST EUROPEANS

French Polynesia's inherent beauty make it a sightseer's delight, but a knowledge of the islands' remarkable history will enhance any visit, for it was on Tahiti's shores that the world's romance with Polynesia began in the late 18th century.

The first Europeans to see Tahiti were the 150 crewmen of HMS *Dolphin*, who had been dispatched in 1766 under the command of Capt Samuel Wallis to search for *Terra Australis Incognita*, a theoretical southern continent that supposedly served as a counterweight to land masses in the northern hemisphere. Many 18th-century theorists believed that without such a counter balance to Europe, Asia and North America, the world would wobble off its axis.

Wallis anchored on 23 June 1767 at Matavai Bay on Tahiti's northern coast. The next morning hundreds of outrigger canoes, which Wallis estimated were rowed by some 4,000 athletic Tahitians, came out to greet the strangers. In each of the canoes was a young woman, nude to the waist, whom Wallis reported 'played a great many droll, wanton tricks' on his lusty crewmen.

The Tahitian men suddenly began slinging stones at the ship, wounding more than a dozen of the British sailors. The *Dolphin* answered with a volley of cannon fire, which sank several canoes and killed more than 50 Tahitians.

Faced with the thunder of cannons and rifles which they had never seen, the Tahitians asked for a truce. When they realized that Wallis had not come to conquer the island but to gather supplies and continue on his voyage, they welcomed the sailors.

Diseases and death

The European sailors who arrived in the 18th century brought along with them diseases such as measles, syphilis and tuberculosis to which the islanders had never been exposed. The effect was devastating. Captain Cook estimated that some 200,000 persons lived on Tahiti in 1769. Forty years later, there fewer than 8,000 left.

Tahitians attacking Captain Wallis on the HMS Dolphin

The noble savage
The French explorer Louis Antoine de Bougainville stayed for only 10 days in Tahiti in 1768, but he took with him to Paris a young Tahitian named Ahutoru, who became immensely popular at the Versailles court as a real-life example of the philosopher Jean-Jacques Rousseau's 'noble savage'. Ahutoru spent a year in France, but died of smallpox on his way home.

Despite the initial animosity, the Tahitians were eager to engage in friendly trade, especially for metal, which the Stone Age islanders encountered for the first time. Wallis' crew soon bartered anything made of iron for fruits, vegetables, pigs, chickens and, in particular, the sexual favours of the bare-breasted Tahitian women. When the sailors exhausted their supplies of iron tools and other objects, they pulled nails from the ship, a practice Wallis soon forbade for fear that the *Dolphin* would fall apart and sink.

Wallis and his crew stayed on Tahiti for six weeks. Although he explored little of the island and did not even visit nearby Moorea, the description he gave on his return to London helped create the island's reputation as a paradise on earth.

A Tahitian woman

THE ISLAND OF LOVE

Unaware of Wallis' visit less than a year earlier, French explorer Louis Antoine de Bougainville anchored off the east coast village of Hitiaa in April 1768. Like Wallis, Bougainville also happened upon Tahiti while searching for *Terra Australis Incognita*. Unlike Wallis, an unheralded British naval officer before taking command of the *Dolphin*, Bougainville was an aristocrat with connections to the French royal court at Versailles.

The Tahitians warmly greeted Bougainville, and although they engaged in rampant theft from the ship, he was so impressed with their beauty, friendliness and supposed sexual freedom that he named his discovery New Cythère, after the home of Aphrodite, the Greek goddess of love.

Based on his travels, Bougainville wrote a bestselling – if not entirely accurate – book about Tahiti, which further glorified it as an island of love.

THE REAL VENUS OBSERVED

By the time Wallis returned to England, preparations were already underway for a South Pacific expedition to plot the transit of the planet Venus across the sun. The observation aimed to determine, for the first time, the distance from the earth to the sun, thus enabling mariners to determine longitude as well as latitude. The task was entrusted to James Cook, hitherto an unknown Royal Navy lieutenant. With him were noted botanist Joseph Banks and Swedish zoologist Daniel Solander.

Sailing in HMS *Endeavour*, Cook arrived in Matavai Bay in 1769 and built a fort on the peninsula, which he named Point Venus. The planetary observations were less than successful, but the three months the expedition stayed on Tahiti resulted in an enormous collection of scientific samples by Banks and Solander, and a detailed logbook description of Tahitian culture by Cook.

Cook made two more great voyages of discovery in the Pacific, anchoring again at Matavai Bay in 1773 and 1777. Although he treated the islanders with respect and hoped they would never be colonized, Cook was killed during a skirmish with Hawaiian islanders in 1779.

MUTINY ON THE BOUNTY

One of Cook's navigators, Capt William Bligh, was sent to Tahiti in 1788 on the HMS *Bounty* on a mission to transport breadfruit trees to Jamaica, where the starchy fruit was to be used as inexpensive food for slaves. Delayed by storms, Bligh missed the breadfruit season and was forced to remain at anchor in Matavai Bay for six months.

Below: Captain Bligh
Middle: painting of breadfruit
Bottom: sunset on Moorea

Discipline soon became slack among many of his crewmen. A few of them lived ashore with Tahitian families, and cohabited with young island women, some of whom became pregnant.

Also, as the Tahitian variety of breadfruit does not have seeds, shoots had to be started on Tahiti and nurtured during the long trip to Jamaica. On the return voyage, therefore, Bligh was forced to both re-establish discipline among his crewmen and devote scarce resources of water to the plants. Neither option sat well with some of the crew, and in April 1789, Bligh's second-in-command, Lt Fletcher Christian, staged history's most famous mutiny.

Below: Brando and Tarita in 'Mutiny on the Bounty'
Bottom: Papeete port

Bligh and 18 of his loyal crewmen were given the ship's long boat, on which they miraculously sailed to the Dutch colony of Batavia (now Jakarta in Indonesia). Christian returned to Tahiti, where 25 of his loyal crewmen chose to remain. Together with eight of the mutineers, Christian and several Tahitian men and women then sailed to remote, and inaccurately charted, Pitcairn Island, where they settled after scuttling the *Bounty*.

After Bligh returned to England, the British warship HMS *Pandora* sailed to Tahiti, rounded up the mutineers who had elected to stay on the island, and took them to London. Only 10 sailors made it back: three were hanged, three were convicted but later pardoned, and four were acquitted.

Bligh later returned to Tahiti for more bread-

fruit, which the slaves in the Caribbean refused to eat. The famous mutiny, however, did spawn profits for the two American writers, Charles Nordhoff and James Norman Hall, who penned *Mutiny on the Bounty* in 1933, a best selling novel that was later turned into a block-buster film starring Clark Gable as Christian and Charles Laughton as Bligh. It was remade in 1962 with Marlon Brando and Trevor Howard. Brando later married his Tahitian co-star, Tarita Tarepaia.

PEOPLE

Of a population of approximately 245,000, some 70 percent are native Polynesians, or 'Tahitians' in the local vernacular. Another 14 percent are of mixed parentage, mostly European-Tahitian and Chinese-Tahitian. About 4 percent are Chinese, many of them descendants of labourers brought to work on a failed cotton plantation in the 1860s. The rest are mostly French, and small numbers of Europeans, Australians and Americans.

The percentage of French and Europeans has been growing since the European Union abolished immigration controls within its member nations.

About half of the population lives in and around Papeete (pop. 120,000). The only other town of any size is Uturoa on Raiatea (pop. 4,000). The Society Islands alone are home to some 86 percent of the total population.

THE POLYNESIANS

The Tahitians are descendants of the Polynesians who migrated across the Pacific in prehistoric times and settled a great oceanic triangle stretching from New Zealand to Hawaii to Easter Island.

The European sea captains who 'discovered' Tahiti in the late 18th century were astounded to find a highly developed society. The Polynesians knew nothing of metal, yet they crisscrossed the Pacific in open canoes for several millennia before Christopher Columbus braved the Atlantic in 1492. They were expert navigators, and were guided by the stars, wind and ocean currents.

A surprising discovery
The whereabouts of the missing HMS *Bounty* mutineers remained a mystery until 1808, when an American whaling ship was greeted at remote Pitcairn Island by young Polynesians who spoke fluent English. Ashore was John Adams, the last surviving mutineer. Fletcher Christian, leader of the mutiny, had died some years before. Although many were later resettled to Norfolk Island off Australia, a few descendants of the mutineers and their Tahitian wives still live on tiny Pitcairn, which has no airport and no regular shipping service.

Below: a Tahitian king
Bottom: Polynesian sisters

Body art

Much to the surprise of the British sailors who discovered Tahiti in 1767, most adult Tahitians had extravagant blue designs etched on their bodies by a process of hammering natural dyes into the skin. The Tahitians called it *tatau* – from the sound of the tapping mallet. The word made it into English as 'tattoo'. In modern times, a renewed interest in their traditional Polynesian culture has led many young Tahitians to revive this ancient art.

Geometrical designs are the most popular but also common are stylized motifs of plants and animals. Numerous skilled tattooists in Tahiti and Moorea offer their services if you decide to get a tattoo while on holiday.

Top-to-toe tattoo

The Polynesians took from the land and sea only what they needed to subsist. To the 18th-century Europeans, they seemed the embodiment of Jean-Jacques Rousseau's theory of the 'noble savage'. There was no written language, yet the Polynesians handed down their knowledge and traditions from generation to generation over thousands of years.

SOCIAL STRUCTURE

Polynesian society was highly stratified from chiefs down to slaves; the latter of whom were sometimes sacrificed to a hierarchy of gods – and occasionally eaten on some islands.

Families consisted not just of husband, wife and children but of grandparents, aunts, uncles and multitudes of cousins. Land and other possessions were held communally. Even to this day, several hundred family members' signatures may be necessary before a parcel of land can be sold.

In the old days, some families with a shortage of female offspring would raise boys as girls. Many of the boys continued to live as transvestites into adulthood, joining a class known as *mahu*, who enjoyed a preeminent position in traditional Tahitian society. Boys are no longer raised as girls today, but homosexuality is an accepted part of Tahitian life, making French Polynesia a welcoming destination for gay men.

The Europeans were most intrigued by the Polynesians' sexual freedom. Young men and women were encouraged to have as many sexual partners as they wished before marriage, and even afterwards, members of the higher classes had certain latitude to dally within their spouses' families. Illegitimate children were readily accepted and raised within the extended family, the foundation of daily Polynesian life.

RELIGION

Pre-Christian Tahitians worshipped at *marae*, or temples made of coral or basaltic stones. These structures ranged from small family chapels to huge temples capable of accommodating several thousand worshippers. Priests would beseech a particular god to occupy *tiki*, figurines carved of stone or wood, during elaborate religious ceremonies.

At the top of the pantheon of gods stood Taaroa, the creator. Below him came several other deities, including Tane, the god of all good; Tu, champion of the status quo; and Oro, the god of war. As a practical matter, the importance of the gods waxed and waned with the success of their human proponents. At the time Europeans arrived in the late 18th century, believers in Oro had the upper hand.

The gods bestowed *mana*, or supernatural power, to all human beings, depending on their social status. The highest chiefs, who possessed the most *mana*, lived such rarefied lives that they used a special vocabulary and were not allowed to set foot on the ground. Only high priests were allowed to touch or converse with the paramount chiefs, part of an elaborate set of rules known as *tapu*, which governed the rigid class system. Anything *tapu*, a word which has crept into the English language as 'taboo', was forbidden.

THE ADVENT OF CHRISTIANITY

Protestant missionaries first arrived in 1797, and although 15 years elapsed before they made their first convert, they eventually made an impact on Polynesian society. Indiscriminate sex, and even

Below: stone totem from the Musée des Îles
Bottom: in church, Papeete

Iorana to you
Although the French greeting *'bonjour'* is more likely to be heard in everyday usage, the more traditional Tahitian greeting is *Iorana*, which means both 'Good Morning' and 'Good Day'.

Below: Papeete town hall
Bottom: Tahitian family

the Tahitians' traditional dances were outlawed – with mixed success. French Catholic priests arrived in the 1830s, and in addition to precipitating France's taking over Tahiti in 1842, they were less critical of traditional Tahitian practices.

Although the Protestants could not outlaw pre-marital sex and suggestive dancing completely, they were successful in converting a majority of the population. Today, Protestants still outnumber Catholics in the overwhelmingly Christian territory.

LANGUAGE

French and Tahitian are both official languages, although French is used almost exclusively in business, finance, government and schools. Tahitian is similar to Hawaiian and the Maori tongues of New Zealand and the Cook Islands.

English-speaking visitors should have little trouble getting around and ordering a meal, since English is widely spoken in hotels, resorts, restaurants (menus are in both French and English), and other tourist-frequented establishments.

ADMINISTRATION

French Polynesia's political status changed in 2004 from a French overseas territory to a more autonomous French 'overseas country'. Although

it can conduct limited international relations within the South Pacific region, the French *tri-coleur* still flies above French Polynesia's own flag. A 57-member local assembly gained increased authority over local matters like land tenure law, civil security, trade regulations and media regulation, but France still controls international relations, defence, currency, justice and internal security. French Polynesians will continue to elect two deputies and one senator to the French parliament.

The new status was the result of efforts by the pro-autonomy party headed by Gaston Flosse, who ruled as territorial president for 17 years. In an election shortly after the change, Flosse narrowly lost his assembly majority – and thus the presidency – to Oscar Temaru, the long-time mayor of Faaa and an advocate of complete independence from France. Upon taking office, Temaru called on France to develop a plan leading to full independence within 10 to 20 years 'when the political, economic, and social conditions are ripe'.

ECONOMY

With about 200,000 tourists visiting the islands each year, tourism is the largest earner of overseas cash. French Polynesia exports some US$200 million worth of black pearls a year, making it the world's largest producer. Most are raised in the Tuamotu Islands, especially on Manihi, but a few farms are also found in the Society Islands. Over-production has seen inferior pearls appear in the local market, since regulations permit only high-quality pearls to be exported *(see pages 55 and 112)*.

The most important contributor to the economy, however, is the French government. Support from Paris has resulted in an artificially high standard of living – by South Pacific island standards. The minimum wage is double that of neighbouring nations, and there is no direct tax on personal incomes.

NUCLEAR MONEY

The artificially inflated economy has its roots in France's nuclear testing programme – or as one

Below: black pearls
Bottom: cruise liner at anchor

Paradise has its price
With few natural resources other than fish in the surrounding sea, Tahiti's economy depends on tourism, black pearls and financial aid from the French government. All this means that the cost of living is very high, in fact higher than most Western countries. For visitors there are few bargains to be had for food and accommodation.

Campaigning against nuclear tests at Papeete, 1995

wag describes it, 'Money that glows in the dark.'

Following the loss of Algeria, Paris decided to explode its bombs at remote Mururoa atoll, in the Tuamotu Archipelago about 1,200km (750 miles) southeast of Tahiti. Some 15,000 French servicemen and technicians began arriving in 1963 to set up the *Centre d'Expérimentation du Pacifique* and its huge support base in Pirae, a Papeete suburb.

Thousands of Polynesians migrated from the outer islands to take jobs in Papeete. While most were grateful for the employment, some reacted adversely to a disparity in pay between themselves and the French, and to the French servicemen's lavishing their pay cheques on young local women. Race riots broke out in Papeete. Many Tahitians had never liked the French presence in their islands, and the riots helped fuel active independence and autonomy movements. The French parliament finally acted in 1977 by creating a Territorial Assembly with control over the local budget. More autonomy has been given over the years, most recently in 2004.

A HIGH PRICE TO PAY

Under President Charles de Gaulle, France exploded its first nuclear bomb over Mururoa in 1966. Despite growing opposition from New Zealand, Australia and other South Pacific nations, France conducted 44 more tests in the atmosphere and 134 underground until 1992, when President François Mitterrand announced a halt to all tests. A year later, the government signed a 'Progress Pact' with the territory under which Paris would provide an 'Economic Restructuring Fund' to compensate for the loss of revenue from the termination of the nuclear tests.

In 1995, France's new president, Jacques Chirac, decided to conduct a new round of underground tests. His announcement was met with international condemnation, including protests by Greenpeace and a tourism boycott by the Japanese. Riots erupted in Papeete, causing the closure of Tahiti-Faaa International Airport and the burning of several downtown businesses.

France conducted six underground tests between September 1995 and January 1996, until Chirac announced that all testing would be halted. The nuclear test facility has since been dismantled and most French servicemen have returned home.

Much of the restructuring fund – which will be halted in 2006 – set up to compensate for the territory's loss of income is being spent to improve airports, build modern docks and terminals for cruise ships, and to fund other projects. Some of it is also being used to develop a commercial tuna fishing industry, once the preserve of a few local boat owners and which has led to the relatively high cost of fresh fish in the local markets.

Below: fresh fish is expensive
Bottom: a good day's catch

NATURE AND THE ENVIRONMENT

The interiors of the lush mountainous islands were covered with ferns, brush, grasses and a few hardwood trees before the Polynesians arrived, and for the most part still are. Likewise with the low, arid atolls, where scrub brush and coconut palms have always predominated.

Of a handful of indigenous plant species, only the gardenia known as the *Tiare Tahiti* is abundant – you will be handed a flower when you arrive at the airport. Another native flower is the five-fingered *Tiare Apetahi*, which is found only in Raiatea's mountains. Otherwise, the flora and

Flower power
Tahitians have always been in love with flowers. You will see them wearing colourful flower crowns when they dance, go out for the evening, or just visit the market.

They also like to place a single flower behind one ear, thereby signaling their availability to members of the opposite sex. Behind the right ear means they are available. Behind left ear means they are taken. Behind both ears means they are taken – but nevertheless still available.

Tiare Tahiti

fauna either arrived from someplace else by natural means or were brought by humans.

The Polynesians, who have always lived near the sea, transformed the coastal plains by planting coconut palms, breadfruit, banana, papaya and other fruit-bearing trees they brought with them, as well as the paper mulberry tree from whose bark they made a type of cloth called *tapa*.

In addition to stowaway rats, the pigs, dogs and chickens the Europeans brought as food sources had a devastating effect on indigenous land birds. The only native bird remaining, the colorful Tahiti lorikeet, disappeared from Tahiti more than a century ago and today can be found only on some of the more remote Tuamotu Islands.

The early Polynesians also planted tropical blooms like frangipani, hibiscus, bougainvillea, poinsettia and other flowers, which add so much colour to the islands to this day. Oil from the sweet-smelling frangipani is blended with coconut oil to make *monoi*, a popular additive used in perfumes and soaps.

In recent years, the warm seawater resulting from the disastrous El Niño phenomenon of 1997–98 has damaged the shallow coral reefs and bleached them of their colour.

WILDLIFE ON LAND

Land-based wild animals consist primarily of a few lizards and skinks, none of them poisonous. The most often seen is the common gecko, which lives in the rafters of homes and resort bungalows. These harmless brown creatures eat mosquitoes and other insects, and so are tolerated by Tahitians.

The bite of the dark brown centipede can be extremely painful, but it also is tolerated because it eats cockroaches, which along with ants and mosquitoes are plentiful in the islands (the mosquitoes may carry dengue fever but not malaria). Another insect, the nearly invisible sand fly, which the locals call 'no-nos' or 'no-seeums', inhabit many beaches and are a nuisance at sunset.

Some 27 species of sea birds nest in the islands, including terns, noddies, petrels and frigate birds.

On land, the noisy Indian mynah, introduced a century ago to control the coconut beetle, outnumbers several species of finch. Chickens run wild on the islands, and roosters serve as unwanted all-night alarm clocks even at resorts.

AT SEA AND IN THE LAGOONS

Although some of the lagoons have suffered from over-fishing, they still are alive with a host of marine creatures. Snorkellers are almost guaranteed to see parrot fish, surgeon fish, angel fish and other colourful species.

Below: turtles are a protected species
Bottom: chasing rays, Bora Bora

Larger and deeper lagoons also attract reef, white-tip, and occasionally, larger sharks. The more dangerous sharks – some 35 species of them – usually patrol offshore. Several species of rays include the giant but harmless manta rays, which add excitement to the scuba diving experience at Rangiroa and Bora Bora.

Hawksbill, leatherback and green sea turtles live in the waters between islands and come ashore to lay their eggs. These endangered species are protected, but nevertheless still hunted by some locals for their meat and shells.

Humpback whales from Antarctica come to mate and frolic in the warm Polynesian waters from July to October. Moorea operators organise whale-watching expeditions during the season.

HISTORICAL HIGHLIGHTS

Prehistory As part of 3,000-year migration from Southeast Asia, Polynesians settle the Marquesas Islands, later backtrack to Tahiti and the Society Islands, then go on to Hawaii and New Zealand.

1595 Spanish Capt Alvaro de Mendaña becomes the first European to find the Marquesas Islands.

1606 Pedro Fernández de Quirós, who was Mendaña's navigator, discovers part of the Tuamotu Archipelago.

1765 English Capt John Byron sails through the Tuamotus in HMS *Dolphin* while searching for *Terra Australis Incognita,* a theoretical southern continent.

1767 Also looking for the mysterious continent on the HMS *Dolphin,* English Capt Samuel Wallis discovers Tahiti and claims it for England.

1768 Tahitians welcome French Capt Louis Antoine de Bougainville. Unaware of Wallis's visit, Bougainville claims Tahiti for France. Bougainville takes back a Tahitian to France.

1769 English explorer Capt James Cook observes the transit of Venus across the sun from Tahiti, and files the first comprehensive report on Polynesian society. Using Tahiti as a base, Cook makes two more great voyages of discovery, charting much of the Pacific.

1773 On his second voyage, Cook's ships run aground at Tautira on Tahiti. He loses two anchors while freeing them.

1774 Spanish ship *Aguila* lands two Franciscan priests at Tautira. They claim Tahiti for Spain but stay only one year.

1789 Lt Fletcher Christian leads a mutiny on HMS *Bounty,* sent to Tahiti under Capt William Bligh to transport breadfruit to the Caribbean as food for slaves. Christian and eight mutineers escape to remote Pitcairn Island.

1797 London Missionary Society ship *Duff* arrives with lay preachers intent on spreading the Gospel on Tahiti.

1819 Missionaries make first convert, King Pomare II, and help him extend his rule over Tahiti and Moorea.

1836 At the urging of Protestants, Queen Pomare IV expels French Catholic missionaries. France sends warship to reverse the decision.

1838 The queen gives in, agreeing to make Frenchmen 'most favoured foreigners', but secretly asks Queen Victoria for British protection. Britain refuses.

1841 French trader gets Tahitian chiefs to request French protection. Queen Pomare IV objects, but France sends another warship to Tahiti.

1842 France annexes Tahiti, Moorea and the Marquesas Islands. Queen Pomare IV retreats to Raiatea. Writer Herman Melville watches the events and later bases his novel *Omoo* on his experiences.

1844–48 The Tahitians fight an unsuccessful war of resistance.

1862 With soaring cotton prices, Irishman William Stewart starts a large plantation on Tahiti and imports Chinese labourers to tend the fields.

1872 Frenchman Julian Viaud visits Tahiti. Under the pen-name Pierre Loti, he writes *The Marriage of Loti,* a best-selling romance.

1880 King Pomare V abdicates his figure-head throne in exchange for a French pension for him and his mistress. Tahiti officially becomes a French colony.

1884 Fire severely damages Papeete, causing the French to prohibit thatch as building material in the town.

1888 The Scottish writer Robert Louis Stevenson stays for two months on Tahiti while writing *The Master of Ballantree*.

1891 Paul Gauguin arrives, spends next 11 years living and painting on Tahiti and Hiva Oa in the Marquesas Islands, where he dies of syphilis in 1903.

1987 France annexes Huahine, the last of the Society Islands to come under its rule.

1903 Eastern Polynesia is incorporated as *Establishments Français l'Océanie,* a French colony headquartered on Tahiti.

1914 After the outbreak of World War I, two German raiders sink the French warship *Zélée* in Papeete harbour and shell the town.

1917 Somerset Maugham visits Tahiti; later writes short stories about the island.

1933 Living on Tahiti, American writers Charles Nordhoff and James Norman Hall publish *Mutiny on the Bounty*, a fictionalised account of the 1789 mutiny.

1935 Clark Gable and Charles Laughton star in Hollywood's adaptation of *Mutiny on the Bounty* – which was not actually filmed on Tahiti.

1942 French local government allows US Marines to land on Bora Bora and build the territory's first airstrip.

1960 Opening of Faaa International Airport brings jet-set tourism to Tahiti.

1962 Marlon Brando stars in a second *Mutiny on the Bounty,* marries his Tahitian co-star, and later buys Tetiaroa atoll.

1963 France establishes nuclear testing facility in French Polynesia. French servicemen and billions of francs pour into the territory, creating economic boom but hard feelings between French and Tahitians.

1966 Under French President Charles de Gaulle, first nuclear bomb explodes above Mururoa atoll in the Tuamotu islands. Forty-one atmospheric and 130 underground tests follow until 1996.

1977 French parliament grants limited autonomy to French Polynesians.

1984 France grants more local self-rule; allows territory have one senator and two deputies in French parliament.

1992 Under pressure, President François Mitterrand announces an end to nuclear testing. Local economy nosedives.

1995 President Jacques Chirac changes policy; announces resumption of underground nuclear tests. Protestors block access to airport; riots erupt in Papeete.

1996 France ends nuclear testing and promises French Polynesia a huge stipend for infrastructure works.

1997 New hotels and arrival of big cruise ships create record-breaking tourism.

1999 Creation of European Union sees increased immigration into Tahiti by citizens of union members.

2004 French Polynesia becomes an autonomous 'overseas country' of France, gaining more authority in some issues. Pro-independence coalition narrowly wins control of local government, and pushes for full independence from France.

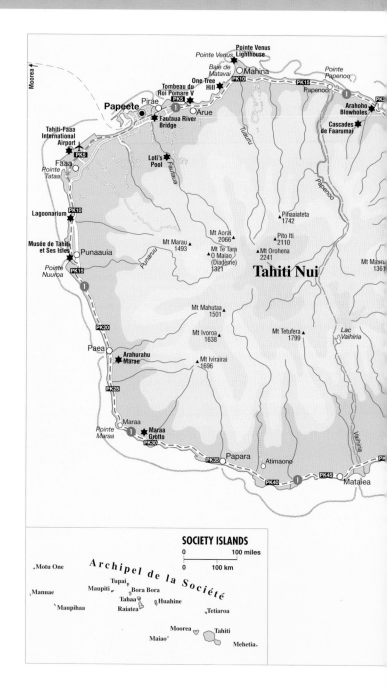

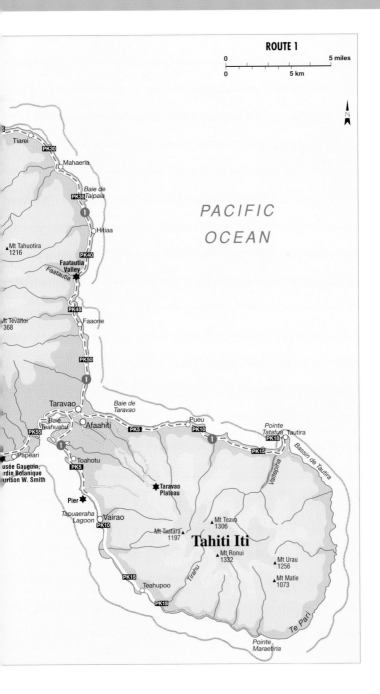

ROUTE 1

Tiarei

PK30

Mahaena

Baie de
PK35 *Taipaia*

1

Hitiaa

▲ Mt Tahuotira
1216

PK40

**Faatautia
Valley**
Faatautia

PK45

Mt Tevaitoi
368

Faaone

PK50

1

Taravao

*Baie
Teahughu*

PK55

*Baie de
Taravao*

Afaahiti

PK5

Pueu

PK10

*Pointe
Tatatua*

Tautira

PK18

1

PK15

Bassin de Tautira

Papeari

usée Gauguin,
rdin Botanique
rrison W. Smith

Toahotu

PK5

Pier ★

*Tapuaeraha
Lagoon*

Vairao

PK10

★ Taravao
Plateau

▲ Mt Teave
1306

▲ Mt Teatara ▲
1197

Vaitepiha

Tahiti Iti

▲ Mt Ronui
1332

▲ Mt Urau
1256

Tirahu

PK15

Teahupoo

PK18

▲ Mt Matie
1073

Te Pari

*Pointe
Maraetiria*

PACIFIC

OCEAN

0   5 miles

0   5 km

N

Map
on page
28–29

Black beaches
While Tahiti has some magnificent beaches, including some of French Polynesia's best surf beaches, all but a handful are made of black volcanic sands washed down from the mountains.

Preceding pages: Bora Bora
Below: Tahiti's high
mountains and
black beaches

1: Tahiti

Although it is by far the largest island in French Polynesia, **Tahiti** was less important in pre-European times than Raiatea, the ancient spiritual and political centre of eastern Polynesia. After its discovery by English and French sailors in the late 18th century, however, Tahiti quickly became the economic, financial, political and cultural hub of French Polynesia.

Although many visitors tend to quickly depart for resorts on Bora Bora, Moorea and other outer islands these days, there is much to see and do on Tahiti, all of it augmented by a fascinating history laced with true-life romance *(see pages 10–15)*.

Papeete *(see page 52)* – the capital of French Polynesia – and its suburbs have grown to encompass the entire northwestern corner of the island and even reach into the steep mountain ridges above the city.

Beyond the reaches of the Papeete, Tahiti is still basically rural and relatively untouched. A tour around the island reveals small villages, well-kept homes amid a plethora of breadfruit trees and bougainvillea, and dramatic scenery beyond every twist and turn of its winding roads.

LAY OF THE LAND

Tahiti covers 1,042 sq km (415 sq miles), about 15 percent of the territory's total land mass. By contrast, the island has approximately 65 percent of its population – about 160,000 people. Some 125,000 of these live in Papeete and its suburbs.

Tahiti consists of two almost round extinct volcanoes joined together by a low isthmus. To the northwest rise the towering peaks of **Tahiti Nui** (Big Tahiti), the larger of the two parts. To the southeast, the smaller Taiarapu forms an appendage to its sister. Taiarapu is often referred to as **Tahiti Iti** (Little Tahiti), or by the French as *Presqu'île de Taiarapu* (Taiarapu Peninsula).

The central volcanic craters of both Tahiti Nui and Tahiti Iti are almost intact, and their outlines are easily seen on topographical maps. Tahiti

Nui's crater is broken only by the **Papenoo River**, which has eroded a winding pathway down to the north coast. Likewise, the **Vaitepiha River** has broken though the Tahiti Iti crater. In both cases, the spines of great ridges radiate from the rim like spokes on a wheel, creating steep valleys in between them.

The mountain peaks that rim Tahiti Nui's crater are almost twice as high as any others found in French Polynesia. The tallest is **Mt Orohena** at 2,241m (7,350ft). Although much lower at 1,321m (4,334ft), the rocky, crown-like **Mt Te Tara O Maiao** (the Diadème) is one of Tahiti's most distinctive landmarks.

Below: headful of flowers
Bottom: Tahiti Nui

DIVIDED BY RAIN

The tropical tradewinds cause moisture to condense over the mountains, often bringing heavy rains to the rugged interior. As a result, most Tahitians live near the sea, either along a narrow coastal plain skirting parts of the island or in valleys between steep ridges radiating from the ancient crater. Modern housing developments also climb the ridges above Papeete and along the northwest coast of Tahiti Nui, granting their residents magnificent views of Moorea some 20km (12 miles) away, across the Sea of the Moon.

Pounded by waves driven by the prevailing

Map
on pages
28–29

PKs mark the way

Poste kilomètres, or PK as they are known in the islands, mark each kilometre along Tahiti's circle-island road. The PKs begin at zero in Papeete and increase as you travel east and west from the city and end at 60km in Taravao. Numbers on the Papeete side of the markers give the distance in kilometres back to the city; those on the other side give the number of kilometres to Taravao, halfway around on the isthmus between Tahiti Nui and Tahiti Iti.

Tahiti Nui mountain road for the four-wheel-drive safari

southeast tradewind, the more rugged – and wetter – eastern side of the island is punctuated in many places by cliffs plunging into the sea. This is especially true of the remote eastern end of Tahiti Iti, which can be reached only on foot or by boat. Elsewhere, the coastal plain is protected by barrier reefs enclosing colourful lagoons.

AROUND TAHITI

Sealed highways run some 120km around Tahiti Nui and about halfway along the north and south coasts of Tahiti Iti. With a few exceptions, these are the only roads outside Papeete and its suburbs, so it is nearly impossible to become lost while on a driving tour of the island.

Most hotels and resorts offer guided half- and full-day 'Circle-Island' bus tours, which essentially follow the round-island road. They will also arrange more adventurous four-wheel-drive 'safari' excursions into the interior.

Since the morning light is much better for photography on the north and east coasts, and the sun lights up the west coast better in the afternoon, the full-day bus tours of Tahiti usually travel clockwise around the island. Capt James Cook went in that direction when he explored the island by foot and rowboat in 1769 – and it is recommended that visitors do the same.

PIRAE AND ARUE DISTRICTS

The flat coastal plain east of downtown Papeete (*see page 52*), which encompasses the Pirae and Arue districts, is the most densely developed part of the city. In ancient times, **Pirae** was a Tahitian village at the mouth of the **Fautaua River**. The modern bridge across the river at PK 2.5 provides a grand view up the Fautaua Valley to the rocky outcrop of Mt Te Tara O Maiao, or the **Diadème**, the only mountain on Tahiti that rivals the grandeur of those found on Moorea.

Star Attraction
● Tombeau du Roi Pomare V

Below: Diadème mountain
Bottom: Pomare V's tomb

Before the river walls were sealed with concrete as part of Papeete's water supply system, lovers would gather at a picturesque pool below a cascade in the valley. In the 1870s, a young French naval officer named Julian Viaud spent two months in Tahiti and later, under the pen name Pierre Loti, wrote *The Marriage of Loti*, a romantic novel based on his love affair with a young Tahitian woman. Part of the book was set at the cascade, which then became known as **Loti's Pool**. A monument to the writer stands by the pool, but it is not worth going out of the way to see.

In the adjoining **Arue** district, the sprawling government complex on the ocean side of the road was the **Centre d'Expérimentation du Pacific**, headquarters of France's nuclear testing operations from 1963 until 1996, when more than 184 bombs were detonated over Mururoa atoll in the Tuamotu Islands about 1,200km (750 miles) southeast of Tahiti (*see pages 20 and 89*).

TOMB OF KING POMARE V

A signposted road turns northward at PK 4.7 to the ★★ **Tombeau du Roi Pomare V**, the Tomb of King Pomare V, in a scenic, lagoonside site that was the ancestral home of the Pomare dynasty. The tomb sits near a 12-sided Protestant chapel, which itself occupies the site of the ancient Taputapuatea Marae, one of the most important Polynesian stone temples on Tahiti. After King Pomare II converted to Calvinism in 1812, he built a monstrous thatch-roof church which was so long – 217m (712ft) – that three ministers had

Map on pages 28–29

Eyes for the king

The Tahitians made human sacrifices at important cere-monies in pre-Christian times. James Morrison, the boatswain on the HMS *Bounty*, was present in 1791 when several bodies were presented at the investiture of King Pomare II.

The presiding priest, Morrison later wrote, 'took an eye out of each, with a piece of split bamboo, and plac-ing them on a leaf took a young plan-tain tree in one hand, and the eyes on the other, and made a long speech holding them up to the young king'.

The Tahitian royal family

to speak simultaneously in order for the congre-gation to hear a sermon. The entire congregation would participate in *himene* (hymn) singing.

The coral-block tomb was actually built as the last resting place of Queen Pomare IV, whose remains were moved there upon its completion in 1879. Queen Pomare IV came to the throne in 1827 and gracefully remained a figurehead monarch from 1842, when France took control of the island, until her death in 1877 *(see page 56)*.

Her son, King Pomare V, succeeded her but abdicated the throne in 1880 in return for a gen-erous French pension for himself, his family and his mistress – thus making Tahiti an official French colony. Pomare V decided that he wanted the tomb for himself and had his mother's remains removed. He then proceeded to drink himself to death, which led to the legend that the Grecian urn atop his tomb is in reality a liquor bottle.

Queen Pomare IV (1813–77) and three kings, Pomare I (1750–1803), Pomare II (1782–1821), and Pomare III (1820–27), are purportedly buried in the **Pomare Family Cemetery** at PK 5.3 in Arue. No one knows for sure, however, since the bodies of high-ranking Polynesian chiefs were customarily spirited away and hidden in caves high in the mountains.

HOME OF JAMES NORMAN HALL

At PK 5.4, just 100m (110yds) beyond the Pomare family cemetery, is an exact reconstruction of the **La Maison de James Norman Hall** (James Norman Hall Home; Tues to Sun 9am–4pm), who along with fellow American Charles Nordhoff wrote the best-selling novel *Mutiny on the Bounty* (1933) and its sequels, *Men Against the Sea* and *Pitcairn's Island*. The two men came to Tahiti in 1920 to write magazine articles. Hall lived in Arue until he died in 1951. In a scene reminiscent of Robert Louis Stevenson's funeral in Samoa half-a-century earlier, Hall's coffin was carried by six Tahitians to his grave on the hill overlooking his home. The present structure, completed in 2001, is a museum dedicated to the two writers.

ONE TREE HILL

At PK 8, the road climbs steep ★★ **One Tree Hill**, which commands a magnificent view down over Papeete to Moorea on the horizon. Capt James Cook gave the hill its name because a single tree stood atop it when he visited in 1769. A gate at the top of the hill leads to the former Tahara'a Hotel (later a Hyatt and now condominiums) built in 1968 as one of Tahiti's first modern resorts. The hotel's lobby was set atop the hill, with nine stories of guest rooms seemingly hanging on the cliff below. At the bottom is the black sand **Lafayette Beach**.

POINT VENUS

Captains Wallis, Cook and Bligh *(see pages 10–15)* all anchored in **Matavai Bay** in the lee of ★★★ **Point Venus**, the flat, sandy peninsula forming Tahiti's northernmost point. Wallis' men set up a trading post under the iron wood (casuarina) trees between the beach and the Tuauru River, which runs through the peninsula, and swapped untold numbers of knives, nails and iron tools for pigs, fruits, vegetables, and sex.

When he arrived two years later, Cook first built a fort on the site of Wallis' trading post, and from there observed the transit of the planet Venus across the sun. The observations were a failure since he did not have the necessary equipment

Star Attractions
- **One Tree Hill**
- **Point Venus**

Below: the home of James Norman Hall
Bottom: Matavai Bay with Point Venus

Map
on pages
28–29

Tahiti time
Despite the optimistic 1867 date carved over its door (*below*), the Point Venus Lighthouse was completed a year later. Locals say it was built on 'Tahiti Time', their name for the slow pace of life here.

*Below and bottom:
Point Venus lighthouse*

to permit the human eye to watch Venus move directly across the blazing sun, but Cook used the fort as his headquarters during the three months he and his crew studied the island.

Today, Point Venus is a public park with monuments commemorating Wallis and Cook, and the black sand beach where Wallis and Cook set up shop provides an excellent view of their anchorages in Matavai Bay. The most prominent building is the 24-m (80-ft) tall **Point Venus Lighthouse**. Snack bars here provide refreshment and there are arts and crafts stands too.

THE PAPENOO VALLEY

East of **Mahina**, a large village on the flat plain adjacent to Point Venus, the coast road hugs the shoreline, hemmed in by ridges descending almost to the lagoon. At PK 13 it passes the **Orofara Valley**, where the government established a leper colony in 1914. Until then, lepers were merely banished from their villages and made to live in the remote interior. The disease is treatable with modern medication, so its victims are no longer banished or confined to leper colonies.

At PK 17, **Papenoo** is one of Tahiti's largest rural villages and makes a marked contrast to the hustle and bustle of Papeete. Shops and government buildings stand along the coast road, and many colonial-style homes with front verandas are nestled among palms, hibiscus and breadfruit trees in the villages behind. Ancient stone platforms in the area indicate that Papenoo was a heavily populated district in pre-colonial times.

The village flanks Tahiti's longest river at the seaward end of the **Papenoo Valley**, the largest on the island. The **Papenoo River** and its tributaries have cut the only opening in the wall of Tahiti's central volcanic crater. The most popular route for four-wheel-drive tours – a sealed road follows the river into the crater from where a dirt track climbs the southern wall – goes through a water-supply tunnel, and then down a cliff-like wall to Lake Vaihiria high on the flank of the southern rim. Another dirt road leads from the lake down to Mataiea on the south coast, making possible an adventurous – and usually quite wet – trek across the island. Surfers consider the waves breaking around **Papenoo Point**, to the east of the river, to be among the best on the island.

BLOWHOLES AND WATERFALLS

The road then makes a sharp bend around a headland at PK 22, where the pounding surf sends water shooting up through the **Arahoho Blowhole**. The road has been widened at this point to include a parking area and an overlook.

A few metres beyond the blowholes a road to the right leads to the ★★ **Cascades de Faarumai**, a series of waterfalls that plunge straight down over cliffs into refreshing pools. The road ends in a bamboo thicket next to **Cascade Vaimahutu**, the island's most easily accessible waterfalls and a popular swimming spot on weekend afternoons. An arduous climb up a slippery track leads to two more falls, the larger **Haamaremare** and the smaller **Haamaremare Iti**.

Below: the Arahoho Blowhole
Bottom: picturesque Cascades de Faarumai

THE LAST BATTLEFIELD

Not all Tahitians were happy about France's annexing their island in 1842, and many fought a guerilla war against the French from 1844 to

Map
on pages
28–29

Ile Nansouty

Lt Max de Nansouty, the highest ranking French officer killed during the Battle of Mahaena, was buried on Motu Teaaupiri, the middle of three small islets on the reef south of Mahaena. The spec of sand and palm trees was for many years known as Ile Nansouty, although, today, the Tahitians once again refer to it by its traditional Polynesian name.

Bougainville's landing place near Hitiaa

1848 (resistance on Raiatea and Huahine continued until the 1890s).

The first important battle was fought on 17 April 1844, when 441 French troops stormed about twice that many Tahitians who were dug into trenches along the beach at **Mahaena**. With help from cannon fire from a warship, the French breached the trenches, and in ferocious hand-to-hand combat defeated the poorly armed Tahitians in an all-day battle. The French lost 15 soldiers; the Tahitians, 102.

Thereafter, the Tahitians resorted to guerilla tactics, which prolonged the war until 1848. The war ended when the French army forced the rebels onto Tahiti Iti and built a fort on the Taravao Isthmus to keep them there *(see page 39)*.

BOUGAINVILLE'S ANCHORAGE

Two more reef islets come into view at PK 36, off the village of **Hitiaa**. These provided scant protection when the French explorer Louis Antoine de Bougainville anchored between them and the mainland in April 1768 *(see page 12)*. A plaque mounted on a boulder north of the river bridge commemorates his 10-day visit. A better vantage point is along the beach at the south side of the bridge.

The aristocratic , highly-educated Bougainville began his career as a French army officer and served as secretary to the French embassy in London from 1745–55. He went to Canada after the Seven Years' War broke out between France and Britain, was promoted to colonel, and served at the Siege of Quebec in 1759. Coincidentally, both Wallis and Cook fought on the British side during the seige.

After the conflict, which is known in the United States as the French and Indian War, Bougainville attempted to create a settlement in the Falkland Islands, whose South Atlantic location he viewed as the gateway to the Pacific. When opposition from Spain thwarted that project, he set off in two ships in search of the mysterious *Terra Australis Incognita (see page 11)*. Like Wallis a year earlier, he found Tahiti instead.

The two islets off Hitiaa did little to break the prevailing east wind, and Bougainville lost six anchors trying to keep his ships from being blown ashore. The Tahitians recovered one of them and took it to the high chief on Bora Bora, who in turn presented it to Cook in 1777.

HITIAA TO TARAVAO

Once south of Hitiaa you will be able to see the mountains of Tahiti Iti off on the southeast horizon. The winding road along this shoreline is one of the most picturesque on Tahiti.

The bridge at PK 42.8 in Faaone offers a splendid inland view of ★ **Faatautia Valley**, one of the most undisturbed on Tahiti. A waterfall cascading into the valley is visible on clear days. In 1957, the Hollywood director John Huston announced plans to use the valley as the setting for a movie based on *Typee*, Herman Melville's novel about his exploits in the Marquesas Islands in the 1840s. It never took off, however: Huston's version of the Melville classic *Moby Dick* had failed at the box office the year before, and as a result, he was unable to secure funding for the new film.

At the beginning of the French-Tahitian war in 1844, the French built a fort at **Taravao**, on the narrow isthmus joining Tahiti Nui to Tahiti Nui, to prevent the guerrillas on the peninsula from

Star Attraction
● Faatautia Valley

Below: people-watching
Bottom: crossroads
at Taravao

Map on pages 28–29

advancing to Papeete. The restored stone structure can be seen through the main gate of the French army training centre, on the right as the road reaches the top of the hill.

Today, Taravao is a sizeable residential community, with a number of shops and a few restaurants along the main road.

Below: Tahiti Iti seen from Tahiti Nui
Bottom: Tahiti Iti peak

TARAVAO PLATEAU

No road goes completely around Tahiti Iti, whose eastern coast consists of rugged cliffs falling precipitously into the sea. There are three sealed roads: one along the north coast to Tautira, another along the south coast to Teahupoo, and a third up to the ★ **Taravao Plateau**, high up on the peninsula's more gently sloping western flank.

At some 400m (1,400ft) in altitude, the climate on the plateau is more temperate than tropical. In fact, ranchers have planted trees along the road and between pastures, making the plateau appear more like France than Tahiti. The road terminates at two overlooks, with awesome views of the mountains and both coasts of Tahiti Nui.

THE NORTH COAST OF TAHITI ITI

Tahiti Iti's north coast road runs for 18km (11 miles) to the historic village of **Tautira**, which sits on a flat peninsula somewhat similar to Point Venus. Although Tautira has little of interest today other than its scenic location, it almost became the scene of international conflict in the late 18th century.

The Spanish viewed the voyages of Wallis and Cook as virtual poaching on the Pacific Ocean, which they had considered their own domain since Ferdinand Magellan first crossed it in 1513. To keep the British out, the Viceroy of Peru sent the warship *Aguila* to Tahiti to claim the island for King Charles III. The ship anchored near Tautira in November 1772, and its captain proclaimed the Spanish monarch to be ruler of Tahiti.

Capt James Cook arrived at Tautira in 1773 during his second great voyage of discovery. Learning of the Spanish visit, he told the Tahitians that they were friends, but not subjects, of British King George III. Cook discovered many islands in the Pacific, but he never claimed any of them for King George III. In fact, he so admired the islanders and their traditional lifestyle that he expressed the hope that none of them would ever be colonized.

During the journey, Cook's ships were unexpectedly becalmed while approaching Tautira, and he lost several anchors trying to keep them from running aground. One of the anchors was recovered in 1978 and is now on display at Musée de Tahiti et Ses Isles *(see page 49)*.

The *Aguila* returned in 1774, this time bringing a prefabricated mission house and two Franciscan priests, who were left behind to both convert and colonize the Tahitians. Despite the friendliness and generosity of the islanders, the faint-hearted priests retired to a stockade and had little to do with their hosts. When the *Aguila* came with fresh supplies in 1775, the priests insisted that they be returned to Peru. The Spanish never returned to Tahiti, but there is a monument to them, on the middle road through the village.

THE MASTER OF BALLANTRAE

Tautira's next famous guest arrived in 1888. Already rich and famous from his best selling novels, *Treasure Island* and *The Strange Case*

Star Attraction
● Taravao Plateau

Silver set
To show her appreciation for Tautira's hospitality during their two-month visit in 1888, the mother of the writer Robert Louis Stevenson sent a silver communion service to the local Protestant church. It is still in use today.

Tahiti Iti coast

Map on pages 28–29

👁 Fishy tales

American novelist Zane Grey, who lived near Toahotu in the late 1930s, was a noted deep-sea fisherman. He set several world records during his stay in Tahiti, among them for sailfish and mahi-mahi. In 1930, Grey landed a marlin that weighed more than 450kg (1,000lbs), not counting the 90kg (200lbs) chunk bitten off by a shark during the 10-hour battle to land the enormous fish. Grey recounted the struggle in his real-life adventure book, *Tales of Tahitian Waters*.

of Dr Jekyll and Mr Hyde, Robert Louis Stevenson was cruising the South Pacific in search of a climate more favourable than Scotland's to his tuberculosis-ravaged lungs.

Stevenson, his mother, his wife Fanny, and her son by a previous marriage, spent two months at Tautira, during which they lived in the village chief's house. Stevenson spent most of his time writing *The Master of Ballantrae*, a horror story set in Scotland.

THE SOUTH COAST OF TAHITI ITI

The picturesque 18-km (11-mile) road through the villages of Toahotu, Vairao and Teahupoo on the south coast of Tahiti winds its way around **Tapuaeraha Lagoon**, the largest and deepest harbour on Tahiti.

A French aircraft carrier and several other naval vessels used the lagoon as their base during the above-ground nuclear tests in the 1960s, and the luxury liner SS *France* anchored in the lagoon in 1974 during her last circumnavigation. Some of the old mooring posts still stand near the shoreline.

This scenic area also attracted the American novelist and short story writer Zane Grey, an avid deep-sea fisherman. In 1928, Grey built a pier into the lagoon at PK 7.3 near **Toahotu** and set up a luxury fishing lodge on the bluffs overlooking the sea.

Scenic Toahotu

FOOTPRINTS AND A MARAE

Look carefully into the lagoon at PK 8.5 and you may be able to see the **Footprints of Maui**. Although formed by natural coral formations, ancient Tahitian legend attributes them to their traditional god Maui, to whom the Polynesians credit many great supernatural feats. In this case, Maui snagged the sun with several ropes, all of which broke except for one fashioned from his sister Hina's pubic hair. Henceforth the sun was tied to the beach, making it move slow enough so that the Tahitians could cook their meals before sunset.

At PK 9.5 is a side road inland where the remains of ★ **Nuutere Marae** are found. Restored in 1994, the ancient temple structure *(see page 16)* was dedicated to a female chief who married into the Huahine royal family.

The road terminates at PK 18 in **Teahupoo**, beside the **Tirahu River**. From there a footbridge connects to a footpath leading along the coast to **Te Pari**, where cliffs plunge into the sea at Tahiti Iti's eastern end. A local guide is essential if you wish to explore this rugged bush land.

Star Attraction
● Nuutere Marae

*Below: the Tirahu River
Bottom: outrigger canoes
at Port Phaeton*

TARAVAO TO PAPEARI

Back at Taravao, turn left along the south coast of Tahiti Nui. On your left is **Port Phaeton**, Tahiti's most protected harbour. In fact, both Port Phaeton and the Tapuaeraha Lagoon on Tahiti Iti are much larger and deeper harbours than Papeete, but they lack two things the capital has: a relatively dry climate and a view of Moorea.

The road skirts around two shallow bays, both used for shrimp farming. On a hill across the last bay, at PK 55.5, stands a private residence built in 1924 by the English writer Robert Keable, author of the best-selling religious novel, *Simon Called Peter*. Like Robert Louis Stevenson, Keable suffered from tuberculosis and came to Tahiti in search of a more agreeable climate. He died just four years after building his dream home.

At PK 52, the village of **Papeari** was the legendary landing place of the first Polynesians to settle on Tahiti, around AD400. Accordingly, the

Map on pages 28–29

Below: exhibit at Musée Gauguin
Bottom: lush Harrison W. Smith Botanical Gardens

Papeari chiefs were the highest ranking on the island prior to the ascendancy of the Pomare clan in the early 19th century. Sitting on a fertile and well-watered plain, Papeari is still one of Tahiti's primary fruit and vegetable growing districts.

THE GAUGUIN MUSEUM

At PK 51.2, ★★★**Musée Gauguin** (daily 9am–5pm) is dedicated to Paul Gauguin, the French artist whose flamboyant impressionistic paintings glorify Tahiti and the Tahitians *(see page 98)*. More of a memorial than a museum, it contains but a few minor Gauguin sculptures, sketches, carvings and ceramics, but it uses photographs, documents, furniture and artefacts to effectively tell the story of the dozen years he spent in French Polynesia. Most exhibits are arranged in chronological fashion. Worth a visit in its own right, the gift shop sells a wide range of Gauguin prints and souvenirs.

The museum occupies a corner of the ★★**Jardin Botanique Harrison W. Smith** (daily 9am–5pm), a lush botanical garden founded by Harrison W. Smith, an American professor of physics who moved to Tahiti in 1919 at the age of 37. He bought these 137 hectares (340 acres) because he knew Papeari had the rich soil and wet climate needed to start a botanical garden – a long-time dream of his. Over the years, Smith imported tropical plants from around the world, so many that there are few native Tahitian plants in the garden. The thick-skin pamplemousse grapefruit, now one of the most popular fruits in French Polynesia, is not of Tahitian origin but grown from seeds he imported from Borneo in 1921.

LAKE VAIHIRIA

After passing a series of headlands descending almost to the lagoon, the road emerges at PK 49 onto Tahiti's largest area of flat land. At PK 48 it crosses the Vaihiria River, which descends down a narrow valley from ★ **Lake Vaihiria**. Tahiti's only lake sits at an altitude of 475m (1,550ft) on the southern wall of the central crater, and cliffs tower another 450m (1,500ft) above it to the crater's rim. The lake – famous for its colony of large fresh-water eels – is about 1km (½ mile) across at its widest point and is at least 30m (90ft) deep at its shallowest point. An ancient Tahitian legend says an eel crawled to the lake from Arue on the north coast and married a beautiful young woman from Mataiea, which explains why the eels have large, human ear-like fins.

GAUGUIN'S MATAIEA

The dirt road at PK 47.6 is the southern terminus of the Papenoo-Mataiea cross-island track *(see page 36)*. The 8km (5 miles) of road to the lake from the southern coast is passable during dry weather but should not be attempted during rainy periods since it fords the river twice and can get flooded.

The somewhat ruffian town of Papeete seemed anything but paradise to Paul Gauguin when he arrived on Tahiti in 1891, so he soon moved to the village of **Mataiea**. The Tahitians still lived the old-style life in rural villages at that time, and Gauguin rented one of their oval thatch huts. He produced several masterpieces during the 18 months he spent in Mataiea.

Gauguin left nothing behind in Mataiea except paintings on three glass doors in his landlord's

Star Attractions
- Musée Gauguin
- Jardin Botanique Harrison W. Smith

Far flung masterpieces The last gallery in the Musée Gauguin devotes an entire wall to reproductions of his masterpieces. It also lists the websites where you can view them.

Lake Vaihiria

Map
on pages
28–29

Beheaded martyr
William Stewart's cotton planting project in the 1860s at Atimaono was not without incident. A defiant Chinese named Chim Soo, now considered somewhat of a martyr by the local Chinese community, was the first person to be executed by guillotine on Tahiti.

Atimaono Golf Course

bungalow, which the author W. Somerset Maugham discovered in 1916 *(see page 101).*

Rupert Brooke, then an aspiring English poet, rented a house on the beach near Mataiea's stone Catholic church in 1914. Although his aim was 'to hunt for the lost Gauguins', Brooke never heard about the glass doors the master had painted in lieu of rent. Like Gauguin, he fell in love with a beautiful Tahitian girl, Mamua, of whom he wrote in his poem, *Tiare Tahiti.* Brooke died of blood poisoning a year later while serving in World War I. Mamua became victim of an influenza epidemic in 1917.

ATIMAONO

The coastal plain is widest at **Atimaono**, an area which is devoted to hydroponic farming and to the ★ **Atimaono Golf Course**, at PK 40, the only links in French Polynesia. This area figures prominently in Tahiti's history, for here in 1862 an Irish wine merchant named William Stewart established a cotton plantation on what is now the golf course and set in motion the creation of French Polynesia's Chinese merchant class.

The American Civil War had driven the price of cotton to record highs, so Stewart's problem was not money but labour. The Tahitians had no interest in working the cotton fields from dawn to dusk, so Stewart resorted to kidnapping other Pacific islanders, primarily Melanesians from the southwestern Pacific, and forcing them to work on plantations in Australia and elsewhere.

When the process proved too slow, Stewart imported 1,000 indentured labourers from southern China, specifically from Canton and Kwantung province. Soon, tthe cotton venture became highly profitable, and Stewart regularly hosted the *crème de la crème* of Tahitian society at *Terre Eugénie*, his lavish manor house in the hills overlooking the plantation. By 1868, however, resumption of cotton production in the southern United States caused a sharp drop in the price of cotton, and Stewart went bankrupt just as quickly.

More than half of the Chinese labourers paid

their own passage back to their homeland, but the rest stayed. Their descendants – many of whom have married Tahitians – now comprise about 4 percent of French Polynesia's population, but they control a vast majority of its shops and other businesses. In fact, Tahitians today call every village grocery a *magasin Chinois* (Chinese store).

When they needed stones for roads and building platforms, Stewart and his labourers went across the road to the **Mahaiatea Marae**, on the lagoon side of a residential neighbourhood at PK 39.2. When Capt James Cook first saw it in 1769, Mahaiatea was the largest and most impressive stone temple on Tahiti. He described it as a terraced rectangle about 100m (300ft) long, 30m (90ft) across, and 15m (45ft) high. Apparently, it had been built around 1760, in a matter of just two years. Little is left of it now except a pile of stones sitting beside a black sand beach.

PAPARA

The largest village on the south coast, **Papara** was the home of Dorrence Atwater, an American who served as the US consul to Tahiti from 1871 until 1888, and who married into the powerful Papara chiefly clan. During the American Civil War, Atwater was captured by Confederate scouts and in 1864, was sent to the infamous

Star Attraction
● **Atimaono Golf Course**

Below: hibiscus
Bottom: the coast at Papara

Map
on pages
28–29

Papara's royal links

Princess Moetia of Papara, wife of American consul Dorrence Atwater – who served from 1871–88 – was the daughter of Alexander Salmon, an English merchant, and Arii Taimai, daughter of the powerful chief of Papara district.

Moetia's brother, Tati Salmon, who later became chief of Papara, struck up a life-long friendship with the American historian Henry Adams.

Her younger sister, Marau, who married and later divorced King Pomare V, was the last queen of Tahiti.

Confederate prison at Andersonville, Georgia, where Union prisoners died of disease and malnutrition by the thousands.

After a few months there, Atwater was assigned to the camp hospital. Suspecting that the Southern government was withholding casualty figures from the Union, Atwater secretly copied the list of dead prisoners. In March 1865 he escaped, bringing to light the horrific circumstances at Andersonville, whose commandant was hanged after the war. In 1875, Atwater married the beautiful Moetia, princess of the Papara district. He is buried beside the Protestant church at PK 36, where a monument stands in his honour.

Otherwise Papara is best known for **Taharuu**, a popular surfing beach at PK 36. The Horue Open surfing championship is held here every July.

MARAA GROTTO AND THE NORTH

The road curves along a series of headlands on Tahiti's southeastern corner, passing the **Maraa Grotto**, also referred to as the Paroa Cave, which indents into the cliff and contains a lake.

Paul Gauguin wrote in his travelogue, *Noa Noa*, that it took an hour's swim to reach the interior wall of the cave. He exaggerated of course, but the cave is much deeper than it appears to be from the entrance. The site has no historical or arche-

*Surfing competition
at Taharuu*

ological significance, but is a popular spot for a cool swim.

North of the grotto, the coastal road enters the west coast districts of **Paea** and **Punaauia**. This side of the island is much drier than the others and for the most part commands views of Moorea, especially from houses on the lagoonside and those now climbing the ridges.

As a consequence, this is the preferred residence of many of the island's European community, making it Tahiti's high-rent suburban area. It also has the most traffic, and high concrete block walls meant to muffle the road noise have replaced the hedges of hibiscus which once lined the entire route. As a result, unobstructed views of Moorea are few and far between.

ARAHURAHU MARAE

A sealed road beside the grocery shop at PK 22.5 leads inland to the ★★★ **Arahurahu Marae** (daily dawn to dusk), the only ancient temple in French Polynesia which has been restored to its original appearance. Although Taputapuatea Marae at Arue and Mahaiatea Marae in Atimaono were more important in ancient times, Arahurahu enjoys a beautiful setting in a small valley bordered by cliffs.

Signboards in both French and English explain the platforms upon which human and other sacrifices were placed, stone pens for keeping sacrificial pigs, the priests' hut, and the raised *ahu* (places for the gods) where chiefs sat during the religious ceremonies.

THE WEST COAST

After passing Le Meridien Tahiti resort and Le Cignalon restaurant, turn seaward at the petrol station at PK 15.1 and follow the signs to ★★★ **Musée de Tahiti et Ses Isles** (Tues to Sun 9.30am–5.30pm), the Museum of Tahiti and Her Islands. Built in the 1970s in a lagoonside coconut grove with an unobscured view of Moorea, this government-owned museum tells the story of the

Star Attractions
● **Arahurahu Marae**
● **Musée de Tahiti et Ses Isles**

Arahurahu Marae

Map
on pages
28–29

islands from their geologic formation through to the 20th century.

Of particular interest are exhibits on ancient Polynesian customs and crafts. The history hall uses photographs and engravings to tell how the islands were discovered and conquered by Europeans. The anchor in the courtyard is from HMS *Adventure*, one of Capt James Cook's ships during his second voyage of discovery. It was lost near Tautira in 1773 and recovered in 1978 during an unsuccessful effort by the British film director David Lean to promote a third cinematic version of *Mutiny on the Bounty*.

The museum is found near the south bank of the **Punaruu River**, the second longest on the island. This area provides a lovely view up the **Punaruu Valley**, and on a clear day, also of Mt Orohena and the rocky Diadème outcrop. The television relay station on the south side of the river stands on the site of a fort built by the French during the 1844–48 war to prevent guerillas hiding in the valley from raiding the coastal villages. Later, the valley was used to grow oranges.

The orange plantations are long gone, but vendors along the coast road now sell wild oranges picked during the July–August ripening season. The area near the mouth of the valley is now an industrial zone and the site of a large quarry that once served as the landfill for Tahiti-Faaa International Airport.

Below: Musée de Tahiti et Ses Isles
Bottom: the Lagoonarium

GAUGUIN'S HOME

After his Mataiea paintings began to produce income, Paul Gauguin bought a parcel of land at PK 12.6 and built a home and studio, where he painted from 1897 to 1901. He donated the property for the school; otherwise his land is now subdivided into suburban house lots.

Worth a brief stop, is the ★ **Lagoonarium** (daily 9am–5.30pm), which is operated in conjunction with the **Captain Bligh Restaurant** *(see page 108)*. Piers lead out to underwater rooms, through which visitors can observe sharks, rays and fish swimming in an enclosed area of the lagoon.

FAAA

At PK 7.8, the fast way back to Papeete is the Rte 5 expressway, which goes east. Rte 1, the more scenic old coastal road, branches off to the north in the direction of **Faaa**, Tahiti's airport and resort hotel district.

In pre-Christian days, Polynesians believed that souls of the dead returned to the ancestral Polynesian homeland, which was always to the west, from where their ancestors had arrived. In the case of Tahiti, they leapt from the cliffs on **Tataa Point** at the island's northwestern corner, thus making it one of the most sacred places on the island. Tataa Point is now occupied by the luxurious **Inter-Continental Tahiti Beachcomber Resort**, which has a glorious view of Moorea.

At PK 5.5 you will be back where you arrived on the island, **Tahiti-Faaa International Airport**. As there wasn't enough flat land on the island to build an airstrip long enough to accommodate modern jet airliners, the solution was to fill the lagoon and reef at Faaa. Before the airport opened in 1960, Tahiti's only air link was via the giant seaplanes known as 'flying boats' of the Tasman Empire Air Line, the predecessor to Air New Zealand.

The winding drive back to Papeete goes through the Faaa district, a majority of whose residents are strong proponents of complete independence for French Polynesia.

Star Attraction
● Lagoonarium

Take the old road
The bridge over the roundabout north of Punaruu River bridge marks the beginning of the four-lane Punaauia by-pass road. For a slower, more scenic, pace, take the old two-lane coast road to Papeete.

Below: the airport
Bottom: Tahiti Beachcomber Inter-Continental Resort

Map below

2: Papeete

Parishioners on parade

Both Tahiti's size and resources had made it a popular stop for whaling ships prowling the South Pacific in the 19th century. At first these ships anchored in Matavai Bay *(see page 35)* near Point Venus, where Captains Wallis, Cook, and Bligh had landed 50 years earlier but they soon switched to a better harbour at Papeete.

At the time the area was sparsely populated swampland, but a small western town soon developed along the waterfront. Papeete has been the capital of Tahiti and French Polynesia since Queen Pomare IV established her residence near the shore in the late 1820s. Pronounced 'Pah-pey-eh-tey', it means 'Water from a Basket' in the Tahitian language. The name is said to have been inspired by a stream that winds through leafy Parc Bougainville, a favourite resting place for Queen Pomare when she lived at the neighbouring Place Tarahoi. Before piped water became a luxury, women used to carry water from this stream to their homes in baskets. *Pape* means water and *ete* is basket, therefore 'Papeete' was coined.

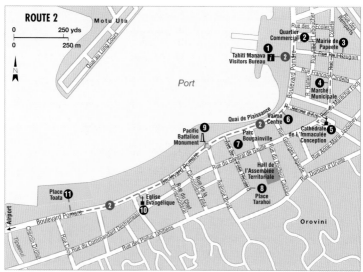

Soldiers filled the swamp soon after the French took over in 1842, making possible the town's growth into a commercial centre.

Most of Papeete's old clapboard shops have been replaced by modern structures today, and its waterfront has been beautified with expansive parks in recent years. Nevertheless, beyond its present-day facade, Papeete still evokes images of its charming bygone days as a backwater South Seas port.

As in the old days, the waterfront is the heartbeat of Papeete, especially the broad, tree-lined ★ Boulevard Pomare, which skirts the harbour. Most of the waterfront has been modernized in recent years. Landfills have replaced the beach, creating public parks and docks for the large cruise ships that tour the islands and the ferries which shuttle between Tahiti and its nearest neighbouring island, Moorea.

International freighters and domestic cargo boats tie up across the harbour at Motu Uta. Until the 1960s, the harbour was protected on its eastern side by a reef islet that was originally known as Motu Uta and a narrow spit of land known as Fare Ute, or 'Sacred House', which took its name from a school for high-ranking children that once stood there. Landfills have covered the reef and islet to create the city's cargo terminal, and Fare Ute is now its industrial zone – hardly worth a visit except for an excellent view over Papeete and its mountainous background.

TOURING THE CITY

The main sights of Papeete are located within a relatively small area near the waterfront and they can be easily seen on foot. Wear sturdy walking shoes and get an early start as the city can get brutally hot in the midday sun. A long lunch is recommended, since many attractions and shops close from 11.30am to 1.30pm.

The ideal starting point for this walk is the Tahiti Manava Visitors Bureau ❶ on the waterfront at rue Paul Gauguin. The bureau stands at the entrance to Tahua Vaiete, an expansive pub-

Star Attraction
● Boulevard Pomare

 Tourist office
One of your first stops in Papeete should be the Tahiti Manava Visitors Bureau, which occupies space in the city's cruise ship centre at rue Paul Gauguin (open Mon to Fri 7.30am–5pm, Sat 8am–noon, tel: 505712). You can pick up free maps and brochures and the helpful staff who speak English will answer any questions you might have.

Papeete vista

Map
on page
52

Calaboosa Beretania

In 1842, a young American named Herman Melville deserted from a whaling ship in the Marquesas Islands and made his way to Tahiti, where he had a ring-side seat to France's taking over the island. For a while Melville was locked up in the local British jail at Papeete, the so-called *Calaboosa Beretania* he describes in *Omoo*, one of three novels he set in the South Pacific.

lic park built with French redevelopment funds to greet passengers arriving on cruise ships, which dock alongside two piers reaching far out into the harbour. The park becomes a carnival at night when *les roulottes* (meal wagons) offer a full range of local food, with everything from steaks and burgers to ice cream *(see page 109)*.

QUARTIER COMMERCIAL

Just cross the boulevard stands the **Quartier Commercial ❷**, the city's historic commercial quarter. Many pearl dealers have shops and offices along its narrow streets, some of which have been turned into pedestrian malls.

Two blocks inland on Rue Paul Gauguin stands the impressive ★**Mairie de Papeete ❸** (Mon to Fri 8–11.30am and 1.30–5pm), the city's verandah-clad town hall. Also known as *Hôtel de Ville* in French and *Fare Oire* in Tahitian, the building is a replica of the Victorian-era palace designed for Queen Pomare IV, which once stood at Place Tarahoi *(see page 56)*. Although constructed in 1990, the building is a striking example of old-style colonial architecture.

Two blocks west, the bustling ★★★**Marché Municipale ❹** (Mon to Fri 5am–6pm, Sat 5am–1pm, Sun 5–8am), the city's thriving municipal market offers a variety of fruits, vegetables, meats, fish and other fresh produce. It is also one of the best places in Tahiti to shop for handicrafts.

Vendors at street level sell *pareu* (sarongs), bedspreads and other local textiles as well as hand-painted items, while those upstairs specialise in handicrafts like shell necklaces, straw hats, baskets and woodcarvings. The entire building is especially lively before dawn on Sunday, when local residents come here to stock up for their traditional midday feasts.

Inaugurated in 1875 on the boundary between the commercial and governmental districts, the **Cathédrale de L'Immaculée Conception ❺** is the city's oldest Catholic church. Local residents still use it as a landmark when giving directions. Inside are several paintings of the Crucifixion.

Stained glass in the Cathédrale de L'Immaculée Conception

ALONG THE WATERFRONT

While the Marché Municipale serves as Papeete's traditional centre for shopping, the four-storey **Vaima Centre ❻** is its modern counterpart. The building houses a variety of black pearl shops, chic clothing outlets, indoor and outdoor restaurants, Papeete's largest book shop, and a multiscreen cinema. On the Rue Jeanne d'Arc side, the **Musée de la Perle Robert Wan** (Mon to Sat 9.30am–noon and 1–7pm) provides an informative introduction to black pearls, French Polynesia's largest export *(see page 112)*.

Vaima Centre sits across Boulevard Pomare opposite ★★ **Quai de Plaissance**, where yachts from around the world moor stern-first in the Mediterranean fashion. Through their masts is a partial view of Moorea's dramatic peaks slashing the horizon.

A two-block stroll along the boulevard leads to **Parc Bougainville ❼**, a shady park named after the French explorer who arrived in 1768 *(see page 12)*. A bust of Louis Antoine Bougainville stands facing the boulevard flanked by two naval cannons extending over the pathway. One is from the *Zélée*, a small French warship sunk at the beginning of World War I when a German naval force under Admiral Graf von Spee attacked Allied shipping in the Pacific and shelled Papeete town.

The other is from the *Seeadler*, in which the

Star Attractions
- Mairie de Papeete
- Marché Municipale
- Quai de Plaissance

Below: the municipal market
Bottom: Papeete waterfront

Map on page 52

German raider Count Felix von Luckner captured 14 allied ships later in World War I. The *Seeadler* was wrecked in a hurricane on Mopelia Atoll in the Leeward Islands. Count von Luckner escaped but was later captured in Fiji.

Absinthe in a tree

Place Tarahoi, centre of French Polynesia's government, was the site of an exclusive planter's club when Paul Gauguin arrived in Papeete in 1891. A platform the club built in a banyan tree, part of which still stands beside rue du Général de Gaulle, was the painter's favourite place to sip an absinthe – until he ran afoul of club leaders and was banished.

PLACE TARAHOI

Behind the park, **Place Tarahoi** ❽ is the centre of French Polynesia's government. In colonial times, Queen Pomare IV lived here in a rather simple house. Tahiti was the domain of a mixed batch of Protestant missionaries until Catholic priests arrived from France in the 1830s.

Perceiving the Catholics as a threat to their evangelical efforts, in 1836, the Protestants asked the queen to expel them. When she did so, Paris reacted with indignation, dispatching Admiral Abel du Dupetit-Thouars to demand that Frenchmen henceforth be treated as the most favoured foreigners in Tahiti.

Queen Pomare IV acquiesced to the admiral, but as soon as he departed she wrote a letter asking Queen Victoria to extend British protection. A local French merchant then managed to get several local chiefs – reputedly by deception – to ask France for protection. Britain refused the Queen's request, and Dupetit-Thouars returned to take control. Tahiti became a French protectorate in 1842.

Place Tarahoi architecture

In 1861, the French government offered to build the queen a large royal palace, but the magnificent building was not completed until 1883, six years after she died. The original palace, since replicated by the Mairie de Papeete *(see page 54)*, was torn down in 1966 to make space for the **Hall de l'Assemblée Territoriale**, where the territory's elected assembly meets.

Star Attraction
● **Eglise Evangélique**

Below: Pacific Batalion Monument
Bottom: the Evangelist church

A NEW PROMENADE

Returning to the waterfront, the four lanes of Boulevard Pomare dip under the roundabout at the foot of Avenue Bruat. From here west a large redevelopment project is replacing the last vestige of Papeete's black sand beach with a modern promenade. Once completed, it should again be home to the **Pacific Battalion Monument ❾**, commemorating a World War II battalion of Tahitians who served in France under Gen Charles de Gaulle. French Polynesia sided with de Gaulle after France fell in 1940. After World War II broke out, the Free French government permitted the US to build an airstrip on the island of Bora Bora *(see page 83).*

EVANGELICAL CHURCH

Crowning the ★ **Eglise Evangélique ❿** is a tall steeple, French Polynesia's largest Protestant church and the mother church of the Calvinist sect founded by the London Missionary Society – whose members arrived in 1797 and were the first Europeans to settle on Tahiti. The group of 18 Anglicans, Presbyterians, Methodists and other Protestants were also the first missionaries ever to leave England. Only four were ordained ministers; the others included a carpenter, blacksmith, bricklayer, tailor, weaver and other tradesmen, whose goal was to turn the 'heathen' Tahitians into industrious, God-fearing Englishmen and women.

They toiled in the vineyard for 15 years before they were able to convert a single Tahitian. The first convert was a high chief they called 'King' Pomare II. In reality, he governed only part of the island and converted primarily to gain their support in his effort

Map
on page
52

to dominate both Tahiti and nearby Moorea. Not only did he win his battles, he ordered all other Tahitians to convert to Christianity.

The present building stands on the site of a thatch-roof church which the missionaries constructed in the early 1800s. Herman Melville described it as the 'Church of the Cocoa-nuts' in *Omoo*, a novel based on his visit to Tahiti in the early 1840s.

Below: the former 'Church of the Cocoa-nuts'
Bottom: Brando's Tetiaroa

PLACE TOATA

Until the city's waterfront redevelopment set out to replace it with concrete and steel, a black sand beach stood across the boulevard from the church. Canoe racing is Tahiti's national sport, and canoe clubs used to store their long, narrow craft here (the government has promised a canoe-docking area in the new harbourfront promenade).Look out for a stone monument containing the twin hulls of the *hokule'a,* a reconstruction of an ancient canoe that sailed around the Pacific without modern navigational equipment in 1976.

Place Toata ⓫, the park at the western end of the harbour, is popular with families. The dance competitions during July's Heiva i Tahiti *(see page 104)* are held here. Next door is the **Office Territorial d'Action Culturelle**, the city's civic centre and public library. Unwind here after your city tour with a drink at one of the park's snack bars.

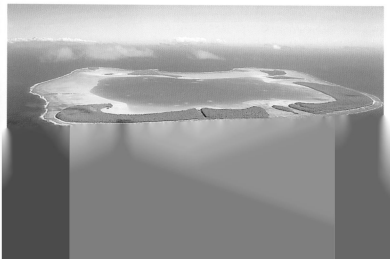

TETIAROA ATOLL

The late actor Marlon Brando began a long affair with Tahiti in 1962, when he arrived to star in the second film version of *Mutiny on the Bounty*. He fell in love with and married Tarita Terepaia, a beautiful young woman from Bora Bora who co-starred in the movie. Tarita bore him two children, Christian and Cheyenne. In 1966, he bought the small, uninhabited atoll of **Tetiaroa**, 42km (25 miles) north of Papeete.

This chain of 12 islets enclosing a multi-hued lagoon once belonged to the royal Pomare family, who used it as a retreat. The Pomare kings sent their daughters to Tetiaroa to lounge in the shade and eat – fair skin and girth being symbols of high chiefly rank in those days. In 1904, the island fell into the hands of Walter Williams, a British dentist, reportedly in return for services rendered to the royal family. Dr Williams had done little to develop his possession, and in 1966, his daughter sold it to Brando.

Brando used Tetiaroa as his personal retreat from the pressures of Hollywood throughout much of the 1970s and early 1980s. He built a rustic resort on one of the reef islets, and a home for himself on another. He turned a third into a wildlife refuge, which he named Bird Island. Although visitors seldom saw Brando, they could enjoy Tetiaroa's tranquility, bask on its brilliant white sand beaches, swim in its pristine lagoon, explore its *marae* ruins, and watch its vast array of migratory sea birds, including frigates, gannets, petrels and boobies.

Constructed of coconut logs and leaves, Brando's primitive resort had few amenities other than a restaurant, a bar, 14 simple guest bungalows and an airstrip. Although it never fully recovered from damages inflicted by a hurricane in the early 1980s, it remained a popular day or weekend excursion from Tahiti or Moorea until it closed shortly before his death in 2004, thus marking the symbolic end of the actor's long love affair with the islands.

Plans are underway to built a luxury 30-bungalow resort, scheduled to open in 2008.

The Brando affair

Marlon Brando's affair with Tahiti came to a tragic end in his Hollywood home in 1990, when his half-Tahitian son Christian shot and killed Drag Drollet, his sister Cheyenne's boyfriend and the father of her unborn child. Christian pleaded guilty to involuntary manslaughter and was sentenced to 10 years in prison. Cheyenne returned to Tahiti and gave birth to a son. She commited suicide by hanging herself in 1995, however, and is buried in Papeete beside her boyfriend's grave.

Following Brando's death in 2004, his ashes were scattered over California's Death Valley and over Tetiaroa atoll.

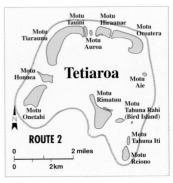

Map below

Moorea bound

3: Moorea

One of the great vistas on Tahiti is not of Tahiti at all. It is of the saw-tooth ridges and dinosaur-like spine of **Moorea**, Tahiti's hauntingly beautiful sister island 20km (12 miles) away, across the Sea of the Moon. Watching the sun set behind Moorea's serrated profile is a scene not soon to be forgotten. 'Nothing on Tahiti is so majestic as what faces it across the bay,' James A. Michener wrote in *Return to Paradise*, 'for there lies the island of Moorea. To describe it is impossible. It is a monument to the prodigal beauty of nature.'

A 30-minute ferry ride from downtown Papeete, Moorea is in some respects a bedroom suburb of the capital. Yet, it has retained much of its old Polynesian charm and all its primordial beauty. It has no town to speak of, and with most houses of its 13,000 or so residents scattered along a narrow coastal plain, it seems like a rural paradise compared to Papeete.

Moorea is also the tidiest island in French Polynesia, thanks to an aggressive anti-litter campaign

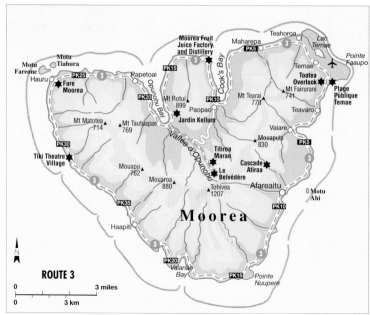

Motu Tiahura
Motu Fareone
Hauru
PK25
Rapetoai
Moorea Fruit Juice Factory and Distillery
PK15
Maharepa
PK5
Teahoroa
Lac Temae
Pointe Faaupo
Temae
Toatea Overlook
Mt Fairurani 741
Plage Publique Temae
★ Fare Moorea
Opunohu Bay
PK20
Mt Rotui 899
PK10
Paopao
Mt Tearai 770
Teavaro
Cook's Bay
Mt Matotea 714
▲ Mt Tautuapae 769
Jardin Kellum
Vaiare
Mouaputa 830
PK5
PK30
Vallée d'Opunohu
Titiroa Marae
Cascade Atiraa ★
Tiki Theatre Village ★
Mouapu 762
Le Belvédère
Mouaroa 880
▲ Tohivea 1207
Afareaitu
0 Motu Ahi
PK35
PK10
M o o r e a
Haapiti
N
ROUTE 3
Vaianae Bay
PK20
Pointe Nuupere
PK15
0   3 miles
0   3 km

by the municipal government. While Tahiti is fringed by black sand, Moorea is skirted by brilliant white sand beaches, which make it a more popular resort destination than its larger sister.

LAY OF THE LAND

Covering 136 sq km (53 sq miles), or about a third the size of Tahiti, heart-shaped Moorea is what's left of a volcano that once towered to 3,300m (11,000ft), according to geologists. The mountain's northern half blew away in a cataclysmic explosion millions of years ago. The top rim of the remaining half-crater has been eroded into the jagged, cathedral-like outcrops that are Moorea's modern trademarks. The tallest now – at 1,207m (3,983ft) – is **Mt Tohivea**, a basaltic thumb with a hole in its peak. The most famous is **Mt Mouaroa**, the 'Shark's Tooth' which appears on the 100-French Pacific Franc (XFP) coin.

Subsequent eruptions in the centre of the crater built the steep and rugged **Mt Rotui** and its stovepipe-topped buttresses, which fall away to fjord-like **Cook's Bay** and **Opunohu Bay**, two of the most scenic bodies of water on earth.

While cliffs line the inside of the crater's rim, sharp ridges radiate from the outside edge, creating sloping valleys between the rim and the sea. A flat, narrow shelf of land bordering the entire coast is home to most of Moorea's residents. Offshore, fringing reefs create excellent lagoons for swimming, snorkelling, diving and boating.

AROUND MOOREA

A sealed coastal road goes for 60km (37 miles) around Moorea. As on Tahiti, *postes kilomètres* (PKs) mark the way, beginning near the airport junction on the northeast corner of the island. The number of kilometres increases from the airport, and reaching 35km (22 miles) going counter-clockwise, 24km (15 miles) clockwise, on the southwest coast.

The airport is located in **Temae**, a district famous for its traditional dance troupes since the days of the Pomare kings. Before he conquered

No poles
Contributing to Moorea's breathtaking beauty is the absence of unsightly electricity poles and power lines. They were quite wisely banned by John Teariki, a former mayor of Moorea.

Below and bottom: Moorea and its clear waters

Map on page 60

Tahiti with the help of the missionaries, King Pomare I spent several years in exile on Moorea. Temae provided the dancers for his court. Although Protestant missionaries later outlawed the Tahitians' suggestive dances, author Herman Melville wrote in his novel *Omoo* that he saw them secretly performed at Temae in 1842.

Pierced by Pai's spear
A Polynesian legend says a Tahitian hero named Pai threw a spear at Moorea on learning that Hiro, god of thieves, was attempting to steal Mt Rotui in the middle of the night. The spear pierced the top of the higher Mt Tohivea instead and set Moorea's roosters crowing, which in turn awakened the people who put a stop to the thievery. Mt Tohivea was thus left with a hole in its peak.

MAHAREPA

Although most municipal offices are in Afareaitu on the east coast, Moorea's main post office is at **Maharepa**, which is also the island's busiest commercial centre. Modern jet-set tourism began on Moorea with the 1961 opening of the original **Hotel Bali Hai**, at PK 5.5. Three young Americans – Jay Carlise, Don 'Muk' McCallum and the late Hugh Kelley – built the hotel and named it after Bali Ha'i, the fictitious island in *Tales of the South Pacific*, James A. Michener's best selling World War II novel upon which Rodgers and Hammerstein's musical *South Pacific* was based.

The trio also constructed French Polynesia's first over-water bungalows, now the most popular type of accommodations on the islands. The **Moorea Pearl Resort & Spa** today occupies the Maharepa site where Hotel Bali Hai used to stand. The surviving partners still operate **Club Bali Hai** in Cook's Bay *(see below)*. Near the Pearl Resort, **La Maison Blanche** (The White House) boutique (Mon to Sat 8.30am–5pm, Sun 9am–noon) occupies one of the best remaining examples of the 'Vanilla Houses', once the most popular architectural style in French Polynesia *(see page 100)*.

Club Bali Hai

COOK'S BAY

One of French Polynesia's most thrilling experiences is to see the dramatic cliffs of Mt Rotui and Mt Mouaroa rising across the dark blue waters of ★★★ **Cook's Bay**. Cruise ships usually let their passengers ashore on the western side of the bay, which has pearl shops, restaurants and hotels, including the Club Bali Hai, which enjoys the most stunning view of any French Polynesian hotel.

At the head of the bay, the village of **Paopao** is one of the largest on the island. It is also home to Moorea's **Marché Municipale** (Mon to Sat 5am–5pm, Sun 5–8am), the island's municipal produce and fish market.

The altar in quaint **St Joseph's Catholic Church**, beside the bay west of Paopao, is exquisitely decorated with mother of pearl. The church also contains a mural painted by the artist Peter Heyman in 1946. The road winds up a hill north of the church, and at its crest is a marvellous view of the hole in the top of **Mt Tohivea**.

A side road at PK 11 on the bay's northwest coast leads to the **Moorea Fruit Juice Factory and Distillery** (Mon to Fri 8am–noon), which produces the popular Rotui brand of fruit juices sold in grocery stores on the islands. The **Gump Biological Research Station**, nearby on the lagoon, is operated by the University of California at Berkeley.

OPUNOHU BAY

Like Cook's Bay, ★★★ **Opunohu Bay** is one of the most beautiful sights in French Polynesia, with jagged peaks towering over its deep blue waters. Opunohu is also much less developed than Cook's bay as the government owns much of the surrounding land. When the second version of *Mutiny on the Bounty* was filmed in 1962,

★

Star Attractions
- Cook's Bay
- Opunohu Bay

Below: Opunohu Bay
Bottom: Cook's Bay

Map on page 60

Long and winding road
The road between the Paopao and Opunohu valleys appears on most maps to be a shortcut from Cook's Bay to Le Belvédère, but looks can be deceiving. The road is only partially sealed, and it makes several time-consuming switchbacks in climbing over the ridge separating the two valleys.

Jardin Kellum

Matavai Bay on Tahiti was still rural enough that the producers could use its shores as the setting for many scenes. By 1983, however, when Mel Gibson and Anthony Hopkins arrived to film *The Bounty*, another version of the story, Matavai was so developed that they had to use Opunohu Bay for the outdoor scenes. The Tahitian extras who rowed canoes out to greet them departed from the black sand beach at the head of the bay.

Part of the shoreline at PK 17.3 near the southeast corner of the bay has been cleared of brush, making it a fine place to stop for photos of Mt Mouaroa. Known as **Robinson's Cove**, this protected area is popular with yachtsmen, who usually drop anchor into the bay and run a mooring line from their sterns to coconut trees ashore.

A short stroll uphill from the cove is ★★**Jardin Kellum** or 'Kellum Stop', indicated by a road sign. In the 1920s, an American couple, Medford and Gladys Kellum, settled on Moorea and built a clapboard house overlooking the bay, where they lived for 65 years. It is now the home of their daughter, Marimari, who by prior arrangement, will guide groups around the extensive gardens containing more than 100 tropical plant species.

OPUNOHU VALLEY TO LE BELVÉDERE

One reason this part of Moorea is relatively pristine is that the Kellums bought considerable land along the east shore of the bay and most of the ★★★**Opunohu Valley**, which begins at the head of the bay. They eventually sold most of the valley to the local government, which uses it as an agricultural research station and training centre. The sealed valley floor road goes through pastureland and passes ponds of fresh-water shrimp.

The road begins to wind sharply as it climbs the sheer crater wall between Mt Mouaroa and Mt Tohivea. About halfway up, it enters a grove of Tahitian chestnut trees growing through the stone courtyard of the ★★**Titiroa Marae**. Signboards explain the role of the *marae* and other parts of an ancient religious complex, which was partially restored in 1967. Nearby are platforms where high-ranking chiefs practised archery, which was a popular sport in old Polynesia.

From its perch high up on the crater wall, the nearby lookout known as ★★★ **Le Belvédère** commands one of the most breathtaking vistas in French Polynesia. The scene sweeps down across all of the valley and the two bays flanking the black basaltic stovepipes of Mt Rotui. A snack bar in the parking lot provides refreshment.

Star Attractions
- Jardin Kellum
- Opunohu Valley
- Titiroa Marae
- Le Belvédère

PAPETOAI TO HAAPITI

At PK 21, near the west entrance of Opunohu Bay, **Papetoai** village is the only settlement of any historical significance on Moorea. The London Missionary Society established its Polynesian headquarters here in the early 19th century. King Pomare I was in exile on Moorea at the time, and after becoming their first convert, launched a successful campaign to conquer Tahiti from Papetoai. The village was the site of a large *marae* dedicated to Oro, the Polynesian god of war, when the missionaries arrived. They tore the *marae* apart and constructed a church on the site in 1822. The octagonal **Temple Protestant**, behind the post office, dates from the 1880s.

The climate is drier on the northwestern side of the island, making it very popular with tourists. The **Inter-Continental Moorea Beachcomber**

Below: Titiroa Marae
Bottom: Le Belvédère

Map on page 60

Map on page 60

*Below: Tahitian-style wedding,
Tiki Theatre Village
Bottom: Club Méditerranée*

Resort, at PK 24, has the widest array of water-sports on the island, while popular dolphin-watching tours leave from its activities centre.

HOTEL DISTRICT

Fringed by one of the better beaches in French Polynesia, the northwest corner is Moorea's hotel district, anchored by the former Club Méditerranée Moorea (now a condo called Fare Moorea), one of the island's modern landmarks, at PK 27. Across the road, Moorea's Comité du Tourisme operates a **tourist information centre** (Mon to Fri 7.30am–noon and 1–4.30pm, tel: 562909). Numerous restaurants and shops line the road while offshore are several *motu* (reef islets).

Beside the lagoon at PK 31, ★★ **Tiki Theatre Village** (Tues to Sat 11am–3pm; tel: 550250, www.tikivillage.pf) is devoted to the preservation of ancient Tahitian customs. Constructed of native materials, staff dressed in traditional costumes explain the old methods of tattooing, cooking, weaving straw mats, carving wood and stone, and making *tapa* (bark cloth) and musical instruments. The village is a popular spot for traditional Tahitian wedding ceremonies, and stages an authentic feast and dance show four nights a week.

HAAPITI TO AFAREAITU

In pre-European times pretty ★ **Haapiti** village was the headquarters of the Marama clan. Although they were early converts to Protestantism, the Maramas allowed a Catholic mission to be built after the French took over in 1842. Today, Haapiti's Catholic cathedral is larger than its Protestant church, a rarity in French Polynesia with its predominantly Protestant population.

Haapiti is worth a stop to take in its view of the 'back side' of Mt Mouaroa. The familiar peaks along the crater rim take on familiar but very different appearances when viewed from outside the ancient caldera. From the Haapiti side, the 'Shark's Tooth' has the same familiar outline but is much less spectacular than when seen from

Cook's or Opunohu bays. There is another excellent side view of Mt Mouaroa from a headland on the south side of little **Vaianae Bay**.

Tahiti comes into full view on the horizon once you round Moorea's southernmost point. At one time the ferries from Tahiti docked at **Afareaitu**, Moorea's largest village. In the mountains above the village, one of Moorea's two waterfalls, **Cascade Atiraa**, drops 32m (100ft) over a cliff into a pool below. A road leads part way to the falls; from there, it is a 20-minute walk to the pool.

AFAREAITU TO TEMAE

Most of the Tahiti-Moorea ferries now land at **Vaiare** in a small bay directly facing Papeete. A hiking trail leads up the valley from Vaiare, over a saddle between Mt Mouaputa and Mt Tearai, and down into the Paopao Valley. Only the adventurous should undertake this trek without a guide.

The coast road makes a detour into the hills behind the **Sofitel Ia Ora** resort to ★★★ **Toatea Overlook** with its monumental view of the lagoon, the Sea of the Moon and the outline of Tahiti. The beach and the lagoon off the resort are the island's best. A dirt road leads from the bridge at the bottom of the hill through a coconut grove to **Plage Publique Temae**, a popular public beach beside the resort.

Star Attractions
● Tiki Theatre Village
● Haapiti
● Toatea Overlook

Below: an 'ahimaa' oven
Bottom: Sofitel Ia Ora Coralia

Map
below

4: Huahine

French Polynesians often use the word 'wild' to describe the island of **Huahine**. By that they mean that this easternmost of the Leeward Islands, 110km (110 miles) northwest of Tahiti, is the least developed of the more visited islands, and that its 5,400 residents are hardly affected by tourism. Indeed, Huahine provides today's travellers with both modern beachside resorts and a prism through which to view a living and breathing traditional Polynesian lifestyle.

Unlike the other Tahitian islands, where chiefs

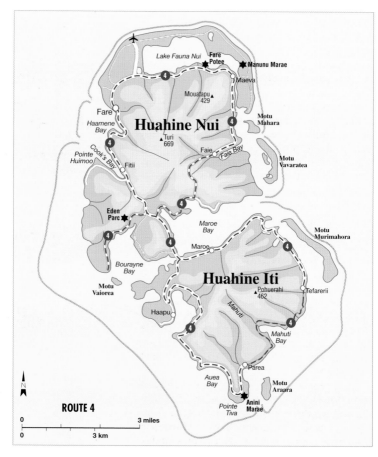

Lake Fauna Nui   **Fare Potee**   ★ Manunu Marae

Maeva

Mouatapu 429

Huahine Nui

Fare

Haamene Bay

Motu Mahara

Turi 669

Faie   Faie Bay

Pointe Huimoo   Cook's Bay   Fitii

Motu Vavaratea

Eden Parc

Maroe Bay

Motu Murimahora

Maroe

Bourayne Bay

Huahine Iti

Motu Vaiorea

Pohuerahi 462   Tefarerii

Haapu

Mahuti

Mahuti Bay

Parea

Auea Bay

Motu Araara

ROUTE 4

Pointe Tiva   **Anini Marae**

N

0   3 miles

0   3 km

lived in the districts that they ruled and often fought wars with neighbouring clans, in pre-European times, Huahine had a central system of government. All of its ruling families lived together in the village of **Maeva** on the northeast of the larger of the two islands.

Here, they built more than 200 stone structures in and around the village, including more than 40 *marae*. These open-air ceremonial and sacred temples were made out of great slabs of stone. Many of them have been restored, which makes Huahine one of French Polynesia's most important archaeological sites.

During the French-Tahitian war of 1844–48, Huahine's Queen Tehaapapa resisted French control of her island and won both naval and land battles against the French. Not until 1897, more than half a century after Tahiti became a French protectorate, did Huahine come fully under the *Tri-Coleur*. To this day, Tahitian is more likely to be spoken on Huahine than French.

Modern Huahine depends less on tourism than on the vanilla, coffee, vegetables, melons and other fruits its residents grow for the market in Tahiti. With relatively few tourists to disrupt their peaceful lives, they also tend to be more friendly and welcoming to visitors.

LAY OF THE LAND

Although not as spectacularly beautiful as either Moorea or Bora Bora, Huahine nevertheless possesses lovely white sand beaches and dramatic bays flanked by thumb-topped mountains. Like neighbouring Raiatea and Tahaa, Huahine is actually made up of two islands, **Huahine Nui** (Big Huahine) to the north and **Huahine Iti** (Little Huahine) to the south, surrounded by a single reef. Together they cover 73 sq km (28 sq miles), about half the size of Moorea.

Huahine was formed by a single volcano and at one time had a great central caldera. The eastern and western sides of the crater either collapsed or were blown away, allowing **Maroe** and **Bourayne** bays to separate the two present-day

Below: hanging out, Fare
Bottom: Huahine from the air

Map on page 68

*Below: not all the roads
are sealed
Bottom: catch of the day
in Fare*

islands. A bridge over the narrow pass between the two bays now joins the two islands, and when the tide is low it is possible to walk across the gap between them. Other mountain-bordered bays cut into the islands elsewhere.

A large flat peninsula arcs around the northern end of Huahine Nui and almost encloses shallow **Lake Fauna Nui**, beside which sits **Maeva**, one of the most historic villages in French Polynesia and site of a large restored *marae*.

Large reef islands off the eastern coast provide land for growing melons and white sand beaches for snorkelling and picnicking.

AROUND HUAHINE

A main road circles each of the two islands, covering a distance of roughly 32km (20 miles), and links the two via the short bridge over the narrow pass between Maroe and Bourayne bays. Most but not all of the two roads are sealed.

Huahine's only town is picturesque little ★ **Fare** in Haaamene Bay on the northwest of Huahine Nui. It immediately evokes images of the era when sailing ships provided the only means of transportation in the islands. Normally sleepy, Fare's tree-lined waterfront still comes to life – even in the middle of the night – when the trading boats arrive from Papeete.

There is a market on the quay, bicycle hire and diving shops. Although of modern construction, the shopfronts are reminiscent of the days when a two-block-long row of ramshackle clapboard shops, many built by Chinese traders in the 1920s, stood opposite the wharf. In one of these shops is the **Manava Huahine Visitors Bureau**, which dispenses useful travel-related advice (Mon to Sat 7.30–11.30am, tel: 687881).

Maroe Bay between Huahine Nui and Huahine Iti is a much more suitable harbour for cruise ships, but Fare sits on Huahine's drier side and is a more convenient location for trading boats en route from Papeete to Raiatea.

There is a sandy beach with a view of Raiatea and Tahaa a few metres north of the wharf. Offshore, waves consistently rolling around the two passes in the reef create two of French Polynesia's best surfing spots.

Star Attractions
● Fare
● Maeva

Hiro's canoe
Polynesian legend correctly recounts that Huahine was once one island instead of two, but it was divided not by geological forces but by Hiro, the same mythological god of thieves who tried to steal Mt Rotui on Moorea island. Hiro sliced Huahine in two by running his canoe across the island.

MAEVA VILLAGE AND MARAE

Heading north and east from Fare, after around 7km (5 miles), the road skirts Lake Fauna as it enters ★★★ **Maeva** village, the old capital of Huahine and today one of French Polynesia's most important archaeological sites. The village itself suffered damage during a cyclone in 1998, but the ancient buildings are made of sterner stuff. More than 200 stone structures – 40 of which are *marae* – many of them dating to the 16th century, have been uncovered along the lakeshore and on **Mataira Hill** above the village. Altogether, 16 *marae* have been restored.

Standing in the lakeside stone courtyard west of Maeva village is one of the most impressive historical structures, **Fare Potee**, a restored meeting house built of thatch and reeds. A **visitor centre** and **museum** housing artefacts and exhibits was recently opened (Mon to Sat 9am–4pm).

Check with the visitor centre about guided tours of the *marae*, including those on Mataira Hill. A sweaty climb up the hill is necessary to reach the restored **Mataira-rahi**, one of the most important temples in French Polynesia, and about 40

Ancient 'marae' at Maeva

Map
on page
68

Take heed

La route transversale across the rugged mountainous centre of Huahine Nui can be impassable during and after heavy rain. Even on a dry day, this steep dirt road can be impossible for bicyclists and dangerous for everyone else.

Below: pearl cultivation
Bottom: Maroe Bay
anchorage

other restored structures, including the houses of priests and the chiefly families. During the French-Tahitian war, the Polynesians built fortifications on the hill, which helped them win the Battle of Maeva in 1846.

LAKE FAUNA AND MANUNU MARAE

Maeva village sits on the narrow, river-like pass through which **Lake Fauna Nui**, also called Lake Maeva – although technically not a lake – flows to the sea. Out in the pass are several restored V-shaped stone **fish traps**, which still work. The ancient traps are clearly visible from the one-lane wooden bridge over the pass.

Across the bridge on the peninsula, the restored **Manunu Marae** is about 100m (300ft) long and stands almost 2.5m (8ft) tall, making it one of the largest stone temples in French Polynesia. The scenic location in a coconut grove beside the ocean is worth photographing.

On the southern end of the peninsula stands a monument of more modern origins, the **Sofitel Heiva Coralia** resort.

MAEVA TO MAROE BAY

The road is sealed south of Maeva to the head of **Faie Bay**. Shuttle boats depart from the north side of the bay every 15 minutes for **Huahine Nui Pearls & Pottery** (daily 10am–4pm), an American-owned black pearl farm and pottery factory out on one of the reef islands.

From Faie Bay the road becomes *la route transversale*, which climbs steeply over a mountain ridge and down to the north shore of scenic **Maroe Bay**. Resembling Cook's and Opunohu bays on Moorea, Maroe is the favourite anchorage of the cruise ships, which ferry their passengers to a wharf on the south shore.

Turn right into the main road at the head of the bay, drive approximately 1km (0.6 mile) and turn left on the Faaua road. This dirt track leads along the north shore of **Bourayne Bay**, the other photogenic bay that cuts Huahine into two islands.

Along the way it passes **Eden Parc** (Mon to Sat 7am–1.30pm), a good stopping place. Here, a lush garden produces organically grown bananas, pineapples, mangoes, guava and other fresh tropical fruit, while a restaurant on the premises sells fresh fruit juices and tasty lunches made from the garden's produce.

Star Attraction
● Auea Bay

AROUND HUAHINE ITI

Hugging the shoreline, the winding road around **Huahine Iti** is much more scenic than that found on Huahine Nui. It is mainly sealed except for the portion between Parea and Tefarerii villages on the southeast coast.

Below: Eden Parc
Bottom: cruising outrigger

All of the island's sites of interest are on a peninsula jutting out from its southernmost point near Parea village. On the tip of the peninsula, **Anini Marae** was not as important as the Maeva Marae, but it enjoys a scenic location next to a lovely beach.

Surfers are attracted to the big waves rolling around the entrance to Araara Pass offshore. The southeast tradewinds can buffet the east side of the peninsula, but on the protected west side, ★★**Auea Bay** is fringed by one of the best beaches and snorkelling lagoons in French Polynesia. Guests are welcome to use the beach and dining facilities at **Relais Mahana** *(see page 124).*

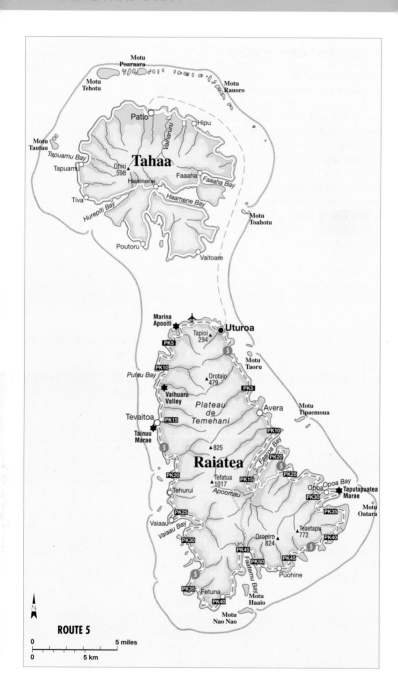

Motu
Poaraara
Motu
Tehotu
Motu
Rauoro

Patio   Hipu

Motu
Taufau
Tapuamu Bay
Tapuamu   **Tahaa**
                    Ohiri
                    598
                Haamene   Faaaha
                              Faaaha Bay
Tiva   *Haamene Bay*

Hurepiti Bay   Motu
                              Toahotu

Poutoru
                    Vaitoare

Marina
Apooiti   Tapiol   **Uturoa**
                    294
          PK5
                              5
          PK10   Motu
Pufau Bay   Taoru
                    ▲ Orotaio
                    479
          ★   PK5
          Vaihuaru
          Valley   Avera
Tevaitoa   **Plateau**   Motu
          PK15   **de**   Tipaemoua
★   **Temehani**
Tainuu
Marae   PK10
          5   *Faaroa Bay*
                    ▲ 825
          PK20   PK20
                              5
                    Tefatua   PK15   PK25
Tehurui   ▲ 1017   Opoa Opoa Bay
          Apoomau   Opoa ★ **Taputapuatea**
                    PK30   **Marae**
          PK25   PK35
Vaiaau   Motu
          Vaiaau Bay   Oatara
          PK30   ▲ Teaetapu
                    Orepiro   772   PK40
                    824   5
                    PK45
          PK50   PK45
          5   Puohine
          PK35   Fetuna
          PK40   Motu
                    Haaio
▲ N   Motu
                    Nao Nao

ROUTE 5

0   5 miles
0   5 km

Raiatea

5: Raiatea and Tahaa

Map opposite

Enclosed by a single reef and lagoon, the islands of Raiatea and Tahaa may lack beaches, but they are the centre of yachting in French Polynesia. Even sailors with limited skills and experience can circumnavigate Tahaa within the relative safety of the lagoon. Those with more experience can brave open passages to Huahine and Bora Bora, both within sight of Raiatea and Tahaa. Unlike neighbouring Bora Bora, there are no luxury resorts and famous restaurants to be found on Raiatea and Tahaa. The upshot is that the islands offer an opportunity to experience a simple and relaxed Polynesian lifestyle that harks back to the old days.

The larger and most heavily populated of the two islands, **Raiatea** is the modern governmental centre of the Leeward Islands and an important stop on cruise ship voyages through the islands. Other than Papeete, **Uturoa**, which sits on its northeast corner, is the only town of any significant size in French Polynesia.

Flower of love
The *Tiare Apetahi*, a delicate white gardenia, grows only on the misty highlands of Raiatea's Mt Temehani and is so rare that it is protected as an endangered species. Legend says a beautiful commoner girl fell in love with a handsome prince but was forbidden to marry him. As she died in his arms with a broken heart, she promised to extend her hand to him each morning forever. Thus, at dawn each day, the flower's five pedals pop open.

A navigable lagoon encircles Raiatea island

RELIGIOUS AND POLITICAL CENTRE

Raiatea, Tahaa and Bora Bora were once ruled by the Tamatoa clan of chiefs, who traced their ancestry back 30 generations to Hiro, the first king of the island (not to be confused with Hiro, the god of thieves in ancient Tahitian religion). As legend has it, King Hiro built a great canoe and discovered both Rarotonga, in the present-day Cook Islands, and New Zealand. Accordingly, ancient Polynesians considered Raiatea, whose name translates into 'clear sky' to be Havai'i, the reputed homeland of all Polynesians. It is said that Havai'i was created by Taaroa, the all-powerful god of creation, and was the birthplace of gods, land and all humanity.

This is not likely, however, given that Polynesians settled in Tonga and Samoa at least two millennia before they arrived on Raiatea, but modern scholars have discovered archaeological evidence linking Raiatea not only to Rarotonga and New Zealand but also to Hawaii.

Map on page 74

Even though the ancient Polynesians settled in the Marquesas Islands long before they backtracked to discover Raiatea, when Europeans arrived in the late 18th century, Raiatea was the most important political and religious island in eastern Polynesia.

The Taputapuatea Marae *(see page 79)*, found on Raiatea's eastern coast, was the most sacred temple on the island then and is today considered the most important archaeological site in French Polynesia. The temple was dedicated to the powerful god of war, Oro, who had replaced Taaroa by this time as the island's dominant deity. According to legend, the birthplace of Oro was Mt Temehani, the flat-topped mountain hovering over the northern part of Raiatea.

Raiatea was also a favourite stop of Capt James Cook on his famous voyages to the Pacific. He make a stop at Raiatea in 1769 and returned twice again in 1773 – when he brought back to Europe a native called Omai – and in 1777.

The people of Raiatea successfully resisted French rule in 19th century, and their island did not become a colony until 1897, when two warships and a force of French marines stamped out all opposition.

Today, the islanders earn their living primarily from cruise ship passengers, yacht charters, agriculture and by working for the government.

Below: Mount Tefatua
Bottom: on safari

LAY OF THE LAND

Separated by 5km (3 miles) of lagoon, Raiatea and Tahaa sit in the centre of the Leeward Islands 40km (25 miles) west of Huahine and about 220km (136 miles) northwest of Tahiti. Because of direct air and ferry connections to Raiatea, most visitors to either island make this island their starting point.

Raiatea is the largest of the Leeward Islands, with a land area of 170 sq km (105 sq miles). Its tallest point is **Mt Tefatua** at 1,017m (3,336ft), from which a long ridge slowly descends to the north until it reaches a plateau atop **Mt Temehani**, at 792m (2,598ft). The relatively flat, often mist-shrouded top of Mt Temehani is one of Raiatea's distinguishing landmarks.

Tahaa is roughly half the size and half as high as Raiatea. It covers 88 sq km (34 sq miles), and its highest point, **Mt Ohiri**, rises to 598m (1,962ft). As is the case with nearby Bora Bora, the mountains are not high enough to create enough rain to make it as lush as the higher islands.

Narrow bays serrate the coasts of both islands. **Faaroa Bay** cuts deep into the Raiatea's mid-section and is fed by the only navigable river in French Polynesia. In Tahaa, **Haamene Bay** and **Hurepiti Bay** almost cut the island in two.

The barrier reef around both islands creates an expansive lagoon that is deep enough to be navigable all the way around Tahaa and about halfway down the east and west coasts of Raiatea.

Neither island has swimming beaches, but there are several sandy stretches on *motu* islets on the reef, especially north of Tahaa where the luxury **Le Taha'a Private Island & Spa** occupies Motu Tehotu. Every hotel can arrange lagoon excursions, which include swimming, snorkelling and picnics.

AROUND RAIATEA

A road skirts all 96km (60 miles) of Raiatea's serrated coastline. As on the other islands, *postes kilomètres* (PK) mark the way, beginning at zero in Uturoa and increasing along the east and west coasts until they end at 50km (31 miles) and 45km (28 miles), respectively, at Faatemu Bay on the

Iriu Notu at the mouth of Faaroa Bay

Map on page 74

Archaeological insights
For an in-depth explanation of Taputapuatea Marae and other key archaeological sites on Raiatea, book a tour with American anthropologist Bill Kolan on one of his Almost Paradise Tours (tel and fax: 662364).

south coast. All of the island's 11,000 residents live in town or along the road.

There was no town on Raiatea until the Rev John Williams, a young member of the London Missionary Society, settled on the island in 1818 and soon thereafter founded **Uturoa**.

Until recently, Uturoa was very much an idyllic South Seas outpost, with a row of quaint shops and a busy produce market opposite a town wharf. Shops still line the main road a block inland, but the waterfront is now dominated by the **Gare Maritime**, built in 2000 with French funds, as the main dock and welcome centre for the cruise ships. The modern building has shops and restaurants, and handicraft vendors sell their wares in traditional-style thatch stalls next door.

The town sits at the base of **Mt Tapioi**, whose 294m (964ft) summit is topped by a radio tower. A four-wheel-drive track leads 3.5km (2 miles) to the tower, where one can glimpse a panoramic view over the town, the lagoon, the sea and Tahaa.

UTUROA TO OPOA

The northeast coast from Uturoa to **Avera** is the most heavily populated part of Raiatea, with houses interspersed with a few general shops all along the road. Huahine on the horizon adds to the scenic view of the lagoon and reef islets.

Uturoa, French Polynesia's second largest town

Around a curve at PK 10, the road enters the spectacular ★ **Faaroa Bay**. Bordered by dramatic jagged peaks, this finger-like bay is reminiscent of Cook's and Opunohu bays on Moorea. A marina perched at the bottom of a steep hill on the north shore is home to one of Raiatea's major yacht-charter operators.

The **Apoomau River** – the locals call it Faaroa River – winds through a cliff-shrouded gorge and across a flat delta at the head of the bay. Rich alluvial soil makes the delta Raiatea's most productive agricultural area. The Apoomau is French Polynesia's only navigable river, and hotels can book boat cruises that travel up it, as well as four-wheel-drive safari excursions into the valley.

After leaving the south side of the bay, the coast road winds around two small bays before entering **Opoa**, an important village in pre-European times. Today, Opoa is notable for its lovely Protestant church. Raiatea is predominately Protestant, partially as a result of having resisted French rule, and thus Catholic missionaries, until 1897.

TAPUTAPUATEA MARAE

At Atiaapiti Point, on the eastern outskirts of Opoa and located in a coconut grove, is the great ★★★ **Taputapuatea Marae**, the most sacred ancient temple in French Polynesia. Built by the Tamatoa chiefs around AD1600 as the home of the warrior god Oro, the main structure is 43m (142ft) long, and the *ahu* (altar) on one end rises to 3.5m (11.5ft) in height.

Legend says that four men were buried in an upright position during construction; their mission being to ward off other spirits and to keep Oro company in his new home. Indeed, Oro was a blood-thirsty god, and several thousand human skulls – presumably sacrifices – were unearthed during a partial restoration of the *marae* in the late 1960s. Archaeologists from the Musée de Tahiti et Ses Isles *(see page 49)* discovered more human bones during a more extensive reconstruction in the 1990s. A basaltic slab standing upright near the *marae* is believed to be the sacrifice stone.

Star Attractions
● Faaroa Bay
● Taputapuatea Marae

Below: Uturoa's marina
Bottom: Taputapuatea Marae

Map
on page
74

Taputapuatea was so important that one of its stones was used in the construction of every new *marae* built in the islands. It faces **Te Ava Moa Pass**, a gap in the reef through which the Polynesians who discovered and settled New Zealand and Hawaii purportedly departed Raiatea. Many apparently returned from time to time to this gathering place for chiefs and priests.

Prime proponents of Oro, the Tamatoa clan had become the most powerful chiefs in the region by the early 19th century. Had King Pomare I not risen to power on Tahiti with the help of Christian missionaries, they would have likely conquered most of what is now French Polynesia.

Below: Raiatea's mountainous interior
Bottom: picturesque Tahaa

TAPUTAPUATEA TO APOOITI

Most visitors turn around at Taputapuatea and return to Uturoa, but you can complete a circuit of the island via the coastal road. The route is extremely winding as it curves in and out of numerous small bays, but Raiatea's south and west coasts rewards adventurous travellers with fine mountain and sea views. Bora Bora comes into view on the northwest coast, adding even more drama to the already spectacular vistas.

Continue past **Fetuna** village, where **Motu Naonao** just across has a nice beach, and beyond Vaiaau to **Tevaitoa**. **Tainuu Marae**, beside the

lagoonside Protestant church at Tevaitoa village on the west coast, is one of Raiatea's oldest temples and one of the few with ancient petroglyphs. The sundial is said to be a navigational reference, and 10 turtles depict an ancient Polynesian game.

The **Vaihuaru Valley** provides a view of the plateau atop Mt Temehani, which seems almost to be sliced into two at this point. A bush track departs Pufau Bay and follows the ridge on the north side of the valley to the plateau – a hike best made with a local guide.

At the north end of the island facing Tahaa, the modern **Marina Apooiti** is headquarters to most of Raiatea's yacht-charter operators. Restaurants at the facility are a good place to fill up before driving past the airport to Uturoa.

> **Fragrant vanilla**
> Also known as 'black gold', Tahaa produces about 70 percent of the vanilla output in French Polynesia. Several vanilla plantations are open to visitors and the technique of planting and harvesting these fragrant pods are explained to you. It is a labour-intensive business as the plants have to be pollinated by hand. The pods then take nine months to mature, after which they have to be laid out to dry for another four to five months. You can buy either whole pods or vanilla in powder form at these plantations.

AN EXCURSION TO TAHAA

Known for its vanilla and melon plantations, **Tahaa** is called the Vanilla Island. Except for those out on its reef islets, it has scant tourist facilities and is of interest mainly to sailors who take advantage of its protected harbours. Reaching 6km (3.5 miles) into the island's midsection, **Haamene Bay** is one of the most popular anchorages for yacht-charters. A mountain ridge separates it from **Hurepiti Bay**, another good harbour on the west coast. Together, the two bays almost separate Tahaa's southern third from its more mountainous north.

Ashore, coastal roads run 67km (42 miles) around the northern two thirds of the island and a peninsula extending to the southeast. The road also climbs over the saddle between the two bays, offering a scenic vista from the top.

Most of Tahaa's 4,500 residents live in villages along the coast. Inter-island ships dock at **Tapuamu** on the west coast, facing Bora Bora. The administrative centre is located at **Patio** on the north coast.

Most hotels will arrange day trips to Tahaa, including visits to a black pearl farm. Unscheduled water taxi service is available at the Uturoa waterfront, and a passenger ferry usually makes morning and afternoon trips on weekdays between Uturoa and Patio, where there is a car rental agency.

Vanilla pods from Tahaa

6: Bora Bora

Visitors from around the world – mostly well-heeled, a significant minority of them both rich *and* famous – are attracted to Bora Bora's deep, multi-coloured lagoon and soft, white sand beaches, over which looms a dramatic, tombstone-like central mountain. The island's almost eye-popping beauty and scores of romantic over-water bungalows make Bora Bora one of the territory's most popular honeymoon destinations.

Although it is by far the smallest of the major islands, Bora Bora has more luxury resort hotels than any other. Most of its 6,000 inhabitants make

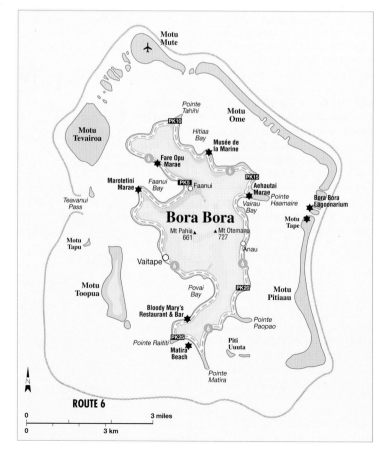

Motu Mute

Pointe Tahihi

Motu Ome

PK10

Motu Tevairoa

Hitiaa Bay

Musée de la Marine

Fare Opu Marae

Marotetini Marae

Faanui Bay

PK5 Faanui

PK15

Aehautai Marae

Pointe Haamaire

Bora Bora Lagoonarium

Teavanui Pass

Vairau Bay

Motu Tape

Bora Bora

Mt Pahia ▲ 661

▲ Mt Otemanu 727

Motu Tapu

Anau

Vaitape

Motu Toopua

Povai Bay

PK20

Motu Pitiaau

Bloody Mary's Restaurant & Bar

Pointe Paopao

PK25

Pointe Raititi

Matira Beach

Piti Uuuta

Pointe Matira

N

ROUTE 6

0   3 miles

0   3 km

Map below

their living directly or indirectly from tourism.

Bora Bora's phenomenal attributes become readily apparent from airplanes landing on **Motu Mute**, a coconut-studded islet on the northern edge of the barrier reef surrounding Bora Bora and enclosing its lagoon. The jagged peaks rising in the centre present a surreal panorama. Visitors are ferried from the airport across the lagoon to their hotels, which means a fish-eye view of the island on the way to the reception desk.

> **Untouched paradise**
> There were no roads, no vehicles, and no electricity on Bora Bora until United States marines arrived in 1942 to build an airstrip and naval base. Bora Bora's lagoon is so big, deep and well protected that it was able to accommodate a sizeable fleet of warships.

AMERICAN HELP

Bora Bora was visited twice by Capt James Cook, once in 1769 and again in 1777. In 1820, a London Missionary Society station was established and in 1886, the French annexed the island. After France fell in World War II, the local population sided with the Free French movement under Gen Charles de Gaulle. When the Japanese attack on Pearl Harbor in 1941 brought the United States into the war, the local administration allowed the Americans to build an airstrip on Bora Bora. About 4,500 US marines built the strip and a large naval base in a matter of months. The facility never saw hostile action and served primarily as a refuelling stop between the US and the southwestern Pacific theatre of operations.

Although giant seaplanes known as 'flying boats' began regular services between New Zealand and Papeete in the 1950s, Bora Bora remained French Polynesia's only airstrip until the international airport opened at Faaa on Tahiti in 1960.

LAY OF THE LAND

Sitting 260km (161 miles) northwest of Tahiti and 17km (10.5 miles) northwest of Tahaa, Bora Bora is but 10km (5 miles) long and only 4km (2½ miles) across at its widest point. As is the case on the other mountainous islands, its 5,500 residents live on or near the coast.

Its dramatic mountain peaks sit atop the western halves of two volcanic craters, one of which forms **Povai Bay**; the other, **Faanui Bay**. The eastern

Opposite: traditional transport
Below: white beaches and deep lagoons

Map on page 82

sides of the craters collapsed millions of years ago, although **Motu Toopua**, a hilly remnant of the rim, remains on the western edge of Povai Bay.

The most familiar of the central peaks is the basaltic slab known as **Mt Otemanu**, which at 727m (2,384ft) is the tallest on the island. On its western flank stands the more regularly shaped **Mt Pahia** at 661m (2,168ft).

Geologists describe Bora Bora as a 'middle age' volcanic island. Most mid-Pacific volcanic islands are slowly sinking back into the sea. In Bora Bora's case, it still has its central mountainous island but also is surrounded by a barrier reef enclosing an atoll-like lagoon. The result is a scenic combination of reef islands, a deep blue lagoon and high mountain peaks.

A chain of reef islets encloses the eastern and northern sides of the lagoon. Some of these now have resort hotels beside their white sand beaches. The lagoon has only one deep-water entrance, **Teavanui Pass** on the western side. The mountains protect this side of the island from the prevailing tradewinds, making the lagoon both a well-protected harbour for ships and yachts, as well as a calm playground for watersports lovers.

Below: Vaitape
Bottom: buffet at Bloody Mary's

AROUND BORA BORA

The only road on Bora Bora runs 32km (20 miles) along the shoreline. It is flat except for two hills on the east coast, so the island can be toured on bicycle as well as by car.

On the west coast, ★ **Vaitape** is the largest village and administrative centre. The airport and cruise ship shuttles land their passengers at Vaitape's dock (where there is a visitor information office), and the pleasant village – only a few hundred metres long – has the island's post office and all of its banks and grocery shops, including the well-known **Magasin Chin Lee**, as much an institution as a general shop.

Facing the wharf, local women sell handmade baskets, grass skirts, shell necklaces and other handicrafts in **Bora Bora I Te Fanau Tahi** (Mon to Thurs 8am–4pm, Fri 8am–3pm). Behind the crafts centre is the *marae*-like **Grave of Alain Gerbault**, a French yachtsman who sailed around the world and settled on Bora Bora in the 1920s. He was on the wrong side of the political fence during World War II and left Bora Bora in 1941 for Timor in Indonesia, where he died. His remains were returned to Bora Bora in 1947.

VAITAPE TO POINT MATIRA

Heading south from Vaitape, the coastal road runs through the residential district of **Nunue** on the north shore of ★★**Povai Bay**, which fills the ancient caldera. Although based on a novel by Charles Nordhoff and James Norman Hall that was set in American Samoa, the 1977 movie flop, *Hurricane*, was filmed in Nunue. This area provides a land-based view of Mt Otemanu's famous tombstone-like southern face, although power lines interfere with photography.

The best, unobstructed view is from the **Bloody Mary's Restaurant & Bar** (tel: 677286) on the south shore of the bay. The restaurant, which frequently gets booked up weeks ahead, is named after the fictional Vietnamese woman in James A. Michener's *Tales of the South Pacific*.

After leaving the bay, the road curves around **Ratiti Point**, site of the venerable **Hotel Bora Bora**, one of the most luxurious resorts in French

Star Attractions
● Vaitape
● Povai Bay

Mathilda's beach
In 1792 a British ship, the *Mathilda*, was wrecked on Moruroa atoll in the Tuamotu Archipelago, where the French were to test their nuclear weapons in the 20th century. One of the surviving crewmen, James O'Connor, married the cousin of King Pomare I. His granddaughter, who was named Mathilda after the ship, married a local chief and settled on Bora Bora's southern tip. They named their property Matira (see page 86), the Tahitian transliteration of Mathilda.

Hotel Bora Bora's over-water bungalows

Map on page 82

Below: a Bora Bora boutique
Bottom: the Lagoonarium

Polynesia (non-guests are not welcome on the premises except by dinner reservation).

Just past the hotel begins long, magnificent ★★★**Matira Beach**, which wraps around the entire southern end of Bora Bora. The palm-bordered area south of the hotel is one of the best snorkelling spots on the main island, although you will have to wade out to the deeper blue water. Two snack bars on the beach offer refreshments.

During World War II, about 400 US marines used block and tackle to wrench two **American naval guns** to the top of the ridge above the beach. Still there, they are a favourite stop on four-wheel-drive safari tours, which every hotel will arrange. An interesting trail to the guns begins near the **Matira Bar and Restaurant**.

MATIRA TO ANAU

The main road makes a sharp curve around a headland near the island's southern end, from where a narrow one-lane road runs down the centre of a flat peninsula to **Pointe Matira**. The peninsula is dotted with private homes, but a public section of Matira Beach on the western shore opposite the **Inter-Continental Bora Bora Beachcomber Resort** is popular with local families, especially on weekends. Also on the western side are several parasail and other watersports operators.

North of the peninsula, both the beach and the main road proceed along Bora Bora's hotel district. Although congested, many visitors elect to stay in this area because the resorts, restaurants, boutiques and other tourist-related businesses are all within walking distance from each other. Among the resorts, the **Sofitel Marara** was built in 1977 as housing for the actress Mia Farrow and other cast and crew members of the movie *Hurricane*.

The road climbs a hill behind the **Club Méditerranée Bora Bora** and then descends into **Anau**, the most traditional Polynesian village on the island. The thin side of Mt Otemanu's tombstone seems to hover over the village.

Boats shuttle between Anau and **Le Meridien Bora Bora** resort out on the northern end of the long reef islet known as **Motu Tape**. Near the resort, a portion of the lagoon has been fenced off as the **Bora Bora Lagoonarium** (open daily 9am–5pm, tel: 677134). Guests can observe and even safely swim with manta rays, turtles and other sealife in the enclosure. Hotel activities desks will arrange visits as it is located offshore.

MARAES AND A MUSEUM

At Pointe Haamaire, about 4km (2.5 miles) north of Anau, the road climbs over two hills. In between them, with a walking track leading towards it, sits ★ **Aehautai Marae**, one of the better preserved stone temples on Bora Bora. Out on the point stands **Taharuu Marae**, a less impressive structure but one with fine lagoon views. More American naval cannons keep silent watch from the hillside.

A land of coconut groves pitted with land crab holes, the northeast coast is the least populated part of Bora Bora. One point of interest is the **Musée de la Marine** (irregular hours; call 677524 to see if the museum is open), a small maritime museum in which French architect Bertrand Darrasse builds and displays models of famous ships that have played a part in French Polynesian history, including Cook's HMS *Endeavour* and Bligh's HMS *Bounty*.

Star Attractions
● Matira Beach
● Aehautai Marae

No lunch break
Bora Bora's relatively desolate northeastern side has no restaurants or other places for refreshment, so take something to drink with you, especially if you are touring the island on foot or bicycle.

Tourists on a canoe trip

Map
on page
82

*Below: American cannons
near Marotetini Marae
Bottom: snorkeller's paradise*

NORTHERN COAST

At **Tahihi Point**, Bora Bora's northernmost tip, a trail leads up to the site of a US navy radar station. This overlooks the lagoon and **Motu Mute**, the long reef island on which the US marines built the territory's first airstrip. Only a portion of the huge runway is needed for today's airplanes. Just as in World War II, passengers are ferried between the airport and their hotels by boat.

If they have not been removed by the time you read this, the modern-day ruins on the northwest coast hillside are that of a failed **Hyatt resort** project. The hotel was to have had a funicular to take guests to their hillside bungalows, but beachside resorts proved to be overwhelming competition.

On the west coast, the road skirts the shore of **Faanui Bay**, which partially fills another ancient volcanic crater. The US Navy used the bay as a large ship and seaplane base during World War II, and the remains of the **seaplane ramp** and **boat pier** on its northern side are still used by local residents. Nearby, between the road and the shoreline, **Fare Opu Marae** has two stones with ancient turtle petroglyphs.

A narrow road runs into a valley at the head of Faanui Bay. Some maps show a trail across the ridge and down to the east coast, but this should be followed only with a local guide.

FAANUI BAY TO VAITAPE

Inter-island ferries and cargo ships dock at **Farepiti** on Faanui Bay's southwestern point. A short distance beyond stands the lagoonside ★ **Marotetini Marae**, the most important ancient temple on Bora Bora. It was dedicated to navigators and was associated with Mt Otemanu in pre-European times. Two of Bora Bora's most important 19th-century chiefs are buried in tombs near the *marae*, which was restored in 1968.

Two more American **naval cannons** sit on the ridge above the *marae*, both aimed at Teavanui Pass, the only entry from the sea into the Bora Bora lagoon. Continue driving and the road soon enters the outskirts of Vaitape and its shops and offices.

7: The Tuamotu Archipelago

A chain of atolls some 1,500km (930 miles) long and 500km (310 miles) wide, the Tuamotu Archipelago presents a stark contrast to the lush and mountainous Society Islands. These low islands – the closest of which is almost 300km (186 miles) from Tahiti – barely break the surface of the ocean and are so difficult to see from ships and boats that the French explorer Louis Antoine de Bougainville called them the Dangerous Archipelago when he sailed through them in 1768. Indeed, their treacherous reefs are strewn with the remains of hundreds of unfortunate vessels.

Another type of wreck lies on the far southeastern edge of the archipelago: the remains of France's nuclear testing facilities on Mururoa and Fangataufa *(see pages 19–20)*.

At one time the Tuamotu Archipelago was a line of high volcanic islands similar to today's Society Islands, but over the eons they have subsided beneath sea level. Only the islets atop the old barrier reefs, which had emerged around the main islands, remain today. The lagoons enclosed by these necklaces of coral rubble and coconut

Lonely islands
Only 41 of the 77 isolated Tuamotu atolls are inhabited, and few have tourist facilities. Known as Paumotu, the people of the atolls speak a different Polynesian dialect than the Tahitians.

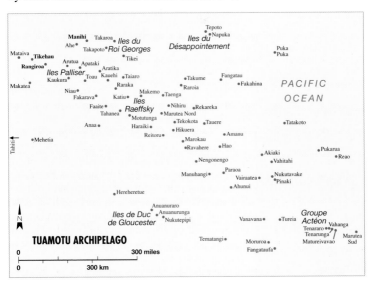

Map on pages 89 & 91

Riding the rip

Swimmers, snorkellers and scuba divers can all 'ride the rip' on Rangiroa, meaning they can literally be swept through the island's two passes – Avatoru Pass and Tiputa Pass – by the 5- to 6-knot tides which flow into and out of the world's largest lagoon. The tides are often accompanied by porpoises, which regularly patrol the passes.

palms seem like giant aquamarine lakes sitting in the blue Pacific Ocean. Because they lie so close to sea level and there are no protective mountains, the atolls are open to the ravages of fierce cyclones and storms.

The clear, clean lagoons are the prime reason to visit the Tuamotu Islands. Stocked with sharks, rays and more than 400 species of colourful tropical fish, the gin-clear and clean lagoons are the prime reason to visit the Tuamotus. The phenomenal array of marinelife makes for the best swimming, snorkelling and scuba diving in all of French Polynesia.

The Tuamotu Islands also produce the bulk of the territory's black pearl crop, an enterprise which has replaced fishing and copra production as the economic mainstay of the archipelago's total population of about 12,000. Visits to one of the Tuamotu Islands' more than 250 pearl farms are on every hotel's list of activities.

Despite occupying an area the size of Western Europe, the Tuamotu Archipelago covers only about 3,800 sq km (1,500 sq miles) of land. The atolls are relatively arid and have limited supplies of fresh water. The climate in the Tuamotu Islands tends to be hotter than that of the Society Islands, especially at night, since there are no mountains to create refreshingly cool breezes after dark.

Divers' jetty, Rangiroa

RANGIROA

Sitting 312km (194 miles) northeast of Tahiti, **Rangiroa** is the largest and most often visited of the Tuamotu atolls. Also known as Rairoa, or 'Long Sky' in the local dialect, it is the world's second largest atoll, exceeded only by Kwajalein in the Marshall Islands.

Measuring some 75km (47 miles) across from east to west and 25km (16 miles) from north to south, Rangiroa's tadpole-shaped lagoon is large enough to accommodate the entire island of Tahiti. It is so long and so wide, in fact, that the islets on one side are not visible from the other. When looking across the lagoon from the shore, in other words, one sees only the 'long sky' on the horizon.

Although the lagoon's vast size means that boat rides of one hour and longer are necessary to reach attractions on its outer edges, scuba divers and snorkellers come from around the world to observe the multitudes of sharks and rays which inhabit Rangiroa's lagoon.

Grey- and black-tipped sharks patrol the lagoon year-round, but the passes come alive with thousands of hammerhead sharks during their mating season from December to March. Huge manta rays searching for mates seem to literally fly through the lagoon between July and October.

PRE-EUROPEAN TIMES

Most of Rangiroa's human inhabitants lived in pre-European times on the western edge of the lagoon, but a hurricane or tidal wave destroyed most of their village sometime around AD1550. By 1800, most of Rangiroa's population had been either killed or captured, or in some cases, eaten by fierce warriors from Anaa atoll to the southeast. Rangiroa's survivors moved to Tikehau and Tahiti for safety, but most returned in the 1820s following the intervention of Tahiti's King

Beach village, Rangiroa

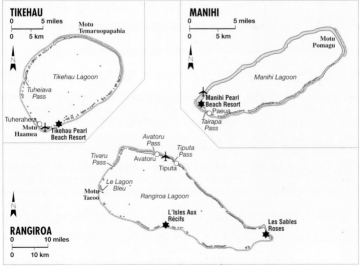

TIKEHAU

0   5 miles
0   5 km

Motu Temaruopapahia

Tikehau Lagoon

Tuheiava Pass

Tuherahera
Motu Haamea
★ Tikehau Pearl Beach Resort

MANIHI

0   5 miles
0   5 km

Motu Pomagu

Manihi Lagoon

★ Manihi Pearl Beach Resort
Paeua
Tairapa Pass

RANGIROA

0   10 miles
0   10 km

Avatoru Pass
Tivaru Pass
Avatoru
Tiputa Pass
Tiputa

Le Lagon Bleu
Motu Taeoo

Rangiroa Lagoon

L'Isles Aux Récifs ★

Les Sables Roses ★

Map
on pages
89 & 91

Pomare I, whose ancestors came from Anaa atoll.

Although the Dutch explorer Le Maire sighted Rangiroa in 1616, the first European settlers arrived in 1851 and established villages beside **Avatoru Pass** and **Tiputa Pass**, the only navigable entries into the lagoon. Protestant missionaries later insisted that all local inhabitants (today numbering about 2,000) move from several small settlements to Avatoru and Tiputa.

Today, the airstrip, hotels, and Rangiroa's only road – a mere 10km (6 miles) long – all occupy the islet between the two passes.

Below and bottom: aspects of Rangiroa's Blue Lagoon

AVATORU AND TIPUTA

At the western end of the main island, quiet little **Avatoru** village is the administrative centre for both Rangiroa and the northern Tuamotu Archipelago. It has a small post office, two banks and public telephone. Typical of most Tuamotuan villages, whitewashed stone walls line its narrow streets, and the steeple atop the Catholic church overlooks everything.

On the eastern end, a **public park** fronts Tiputa Pass, where porpoises usually frolic during the early mornings and late afternoons. Unscheduled boats go back and forth from a wharf to **Tiputa** village, another typically Tuamotuan settlement located on the eastern side of the pass. Like Avatoru, it has a whitewashed Catholic church.

MAIN SIGHTS

Rangiroa's prime attractions lie on the edges of the lagoon, all at least an hour's boat ride from the hotels, all of which will arrange guided tours, the only practical way to get there.

Enclosed by reef islets on the western end, ★ **Le Lagon Bleu** (the Blue Lagoon) is a small lagoon within the larger main lagoon. Brilliant white sand beaches ring its warm, shallow waters, and **Motu Taeoo**, one of several reef islets that are official bird sanctuaries, is a short walk away.

On Rangiroa's eastern end, near Motu Vahituri and fringing the inner reef is ★★ **Les Sables**

Roses or the 'The Pink Sands' – which get their unusual colour from foraminifera deposits that glow with reflected pink light when the sun shines. The lagoon is narrowest at its eastern extremity, which makes the sands there more scenic than at other location where it is so wide that only the horizon is visible in the distance.

On the southern side, ★ **L'Isle Aux Récifs** (The Reef Islands), also known as Motu Ai Ai, are notable for fossilized coral outcrops called *feo*, which resemble castles. Snorkelling off the islet is among the best on Rangiroa.

Star Attractions
● Le Lagon Bleu
● Les Sables Roses
● L'Isle Aux Récifs

MANIHI

French Polynesia's black pearl industry began in the late 1960s on the island of **Manihi**, which is today the territory's leading producer of black pearls. More than 60 pearl farms stand on stilts along the shore and over numerous coral heads dotting this relatively shallow lagoon, which lie some 150km (93 miles) east of Rangiroa and 520km (312 miles) northeast of Tahiti.

In addition to swimming, snorkelling and scuba diving in the clear lagoon, visiting a pearl farm is a major activity for visitors to Manihi.

Manihi's 800 residents are likely wear more pearls per capita than the population of any other island. Most of them work in the pearl industry

Below: pearl farming, Manihi
Bottom: picture perfect Les Sables Roses beach

Map on page 89 & 91

Bring money
Manihi and Tikehau both have post offices, but neither has a bank. The two resort hotels on the islands accept all major credit cards, but bring local currency if you intend to shop in the villages.

Opposite: paradise found
Below: Manihi Pearl Beach Resort

and live in **Paeua**, a relatively wealthy village sitting on the island's southwestern corner beside **Tairapa Pass**, the only navigable entry into the lagoon. One of the village's main attractions is a huge tree, under which local residents gather to watch the comings and goings at the wharf. The airport and the **Manihi Pearl Beach Resort**, Manihi's only hotel, are on a larger islet to the west of Tairapa Pass.

Measuring 30km (19 miles) long by 5.6km (3.5 miles) wide, the Manihi lagoon is much smaller than Rangiroa's and is better known to scuba divers for its abundant tropical fish than for sharks and rays. Tairapa Pass is also wider and shallower than Rangiroa's, but it has a strong enough current for snorkellers and scuba divers to ride the rip.

TIKEHAU

Although it sits just 15km (9 miles) west of Rangiroa, **Tikehau** offers a more remote experience than its larger sister island. Its nearly circular lagoon is 26km (16 miles) across at its widest point, small enough so that all of the encircling reef islets are visible from the lagoon shore, which adds a scenic beauty lacking at both Rangiroa and Manihi.

Although the lagoon is no more than 30m (100ft) deep, it has more fish per square kilometre than any other lagoon in the Tuamotus. (Tikehau's residents earn their livelihoods primarily by fishing and shipping their catch to the markets in Papeete.) On the other hand, Tikehau lacks the many sharks and manta rays that make Rangiroa a scuba diver's delight. Nor does a strong rip tide run through **Tuheiava Pass**, the only entrance into the lagoon.

Most of Tikehau's 400 residents live in the village of **Tuherahera**, which shares a large *motu* on the south side of the lagoon with the airport. Tuherahera is famous for its many flowers adorning the large yards around its neat concrete and clapboard houses. The village has a bakery, three grocery shops, a handicraft shop and a few pensions. **Tikehau Pearl Beach Resort**, the island's only luxury hotel, occupies a small islet 15 minutes by boat from Tuherahera.

Art and Architecture

Beginning in the late 1970s, Tahiti and French Polynesia have been experiencing a cultural renaissance, resulting in increased awareness on the part of Tahitians of their traditional *Maohi* heritage. ('Maohi' is the Tahitian version of the New Zealand word *Maori*, or 'Polynesian' in English.)

The movement's cultural side is best expressed by the Tiki Theatre Village on Moorea *(see page 66)*, a showplace of the ancient Tahitian arts and crafts. But there is also a political side to the heightened awareness as evidenced by the success of the pro-autonomy party government, which was in power for 20 years, and its defeat in 2004 by a coalition of parties favouring full independence from France.

Although most Tahitians speak French and many wear the hippest fashions from Paris and listen to the latest rock music from New York, the reawakening of Polynesian pride is evident to visitors in the traditional tattoos that many young Tahitians now sport. Some young Tahitian men also are letting their wavy black hair grow long, as their ancestors did when captains Wallis, Cook and Bougainville visited them in the 1760s.

TAHITIAN ARTS AND CRAFTS

Traditional Tahitian tattoos feature the simple geometric designs which have dominated Polynesian art for more than two millennia. Each clan had its own motif, which was etched not only on human skin but also painted, using natural dyes, on *tapa*. This is a type of cloth made by pounding the bark of the paper mulberry tree, called *aute*, into thin sheets. Imported cloth, however, has made *tapa* a rapidly disappearing craft.

Pareu are brightly patterned sarongs worn by both men and women. Many are now imported but look out for local designers' work.

The Polynesians were also fine carvers of wood and stone, particularly of intricate *tiki*, figurines which adorned their *marae*, or places of worship constructed of coral and basaltic stone. When the

Opposite: wood sculpture, Moorea
Below: the real thing
Bottom: tiki images

fundamentalist Protestant missionaries arrived, they ordered these pagan *tiki* to be destroyed throughout the Society Islands. Only in the Marquesas Islands has the art of carving *tiki* survived to the present day.

The Polynesians also used coconut and *pandanus* leaves to weave baskets and mats, which they still do, primarily in the outer islands. Although they made pottery in ancient times, this skill had completely died out in Tahiti by the 18th century.

PAUL GAUGUIN

The first European artist to paint Tahiti was William Hodges, who accompanied Capt James Cook on his second voyage to Tahiti in 1773–74. Masterfully depicting the glorious colour and light of the Pacific, Hodges' realistic land- and seascapes were the late 18th-century equivalent of today's television images from outer space.

Art in Tahiti, however, will always be associated with Paul Gauguin, the French painter who lived and worked in the islands from 1891 until his untimely death in 1903.

Born in 1848, Gauguin was a marginally successful Parisian painter when he quit his full-time job as a stockbroker and abandoned his wife and six children to devote himself to his art full time. He went first to Martinique in the Caribbean but

Below: sculpture of the artist in the Musée Gauguin
Bottom: 'Femmes de Tahiti' (detail), by Paul Gauguin (1891)

soon tired of it and moved to Papeete in June 1891 when he was 43 years old.

Gauguin led a troublesome Tahitian existence almost from the moment he arrived. He frequently quarrelled with the local French officials, he was constantly in debt, he was addicted to opium, and he suffered from many illnesses, including syphilis, which eventually killed him.

Gauguin was happiest and most productive when he lived in Mataiea, on Tahiti's south coast, from 1891 to 1893. Out of his rented thatch hut came such masterpieces as *Under the Pandanus* and *Rêverie*. He also painted the three glass doors in his landlord's bungalow, which were discovered in 1916 by Somerset Maugham. Maugham bought one of the doors and kept it his French Riviera home until shortly before his death.

After his Mataiea paintings sold in Paris, Gauguin built a house and studio in Punaauia on Tahiti's west coast. He worked there from 1895 until 1901, producing such works as *Two Tahitian Women*, *Faa Iheine*, and *Where Do We Come From? What are We? Where are We Going?*

Unfortunately, he squandered his money and continued to have difficulties with the local officials. In 1901, he deserted Tahiti and moved to Hiva Oa in the Marquesas, where he helped the locals oppose the colonial administration and the church. He died there two years later and is buried near the village of Atuona.

Gauguin's bold and colourful impressionistic depiction of the islands has influenced many other painters who have lived in the islands, including William Leeteg, François Ravello, Michell Dallet and the Hawaiian artist Bobby Holcomb, who lived and worked on Huahine until his death in 1991. Their works are occasionally offered for sale by art galleries in both Papeete and Moorea.

> **Gauguin's first mistress**
> When Paul Gauguin moved to Mataiea on Tahiti's south coast in 1891, a Tahitian woman asked him what he was doing. He replied that he was looking for a young girl, meaning a model. Misunderstanding Gauguin, the woman offered the sexual favours of her 13-year-old daughter, Tehaamana. The first of Gauguin's many young Tahitian mistresses, Tehaamana appears in several of his masterpieces.

Boutique Gauguin, Bora Bora

FROM THATCH TO TIN

Prior to the arrival of the Europeans, the islanders built their houses and public buildings from natural materials. Most consisted of coconut poles supporting tall, peaked roofs of tree limbs lashed together with rope made of coconut fibre and covered by layers of coconut or pandanus leaf thatch.

These so-called leaf roofs were ideal for the tropical climate. On the one hand they kept out sunlight and rain. On the other, they let hot air escape during the day but retained warm air at night. But they were also highly flammable, and after a fire raged through Papeete in 1884, local officials outlawed thatch as a building material within the town limits.

Although most private homes today are plywood structures with tin roofs, the early European settlers constructed their clapboard houses with more flair. Beginning in the early 20th century, their preferred architectural style took advantage of natural ventilation by the use of high ceilings, tall windows, central hallways and broad verandahs. These became known as 'vanilla houses' in French Polynesia because the owners of vanilla plantations often designed their homes in this fashion.

You will pass a few of these charming vanilla houses as you tour the islands. One of the best examples open to the public is La Maison Blanche on Moorea *(see page 62)*. Although it is a recent reconstruction, the James Norman Hall Home on Tahiti is another good example *(see page 34)*.

High ceilings, tall windows and wrap-around verandahs were also used extensively in public

Below: thatch is now much more common in tourist complexes than Tahitian dwellings
Bottom: La Maison Blanche on Moorea

buildings during the colonial era, but few of these remain. The best example is the Mairie de Papeete, the city's town hall replica of the palace built for Queen Pomare IV *(see page 54)*.

Christian churches built of coral block are unique to the South Pacific islands. Their thick, whitewashed walls make them relatively cool places to worship even on the hottest days. Many of them remain in the rural villages.

Literature and Music

Paul Gauguin is best known as a painter, but he also contributed to an expansive body of literature about the islands with *Noa Noa*, a travelogue published in 1928. It is one of many books in which famous writers have brought Tahiti's romance and beauty to the rest of the world.

FAMOUS WRITERS

The first was Herman Melville, the American novelist who in the early 1840s first deserted a whaling ship in the Marquesas and then participated in a minor mutiny on Tahiti. His first novel, *Typee*, was a fictionalized account of his Marquesan adventures. His second, *Omoo*, was based on his experiences on Tahiti and Moorea during the French takeover in 1842, including his brief stay in the 'Calaboosa Beretania' *(see page 54)*. Melville's greatest work, the classic whaling tale *Moby Dick*, was set in the South Pacific.

Next came Julian Viaud, the young French midshipman who spent two months on Tahiti in the late 1870s and who, under the pen name Pierre Loti, wrote *The Marriage of Loti*, a novel based on his own love affair with a young Tahitian woman. The book help convince Paul Gauguin to come to French Polynesia.

Somerset Maugham visited Tahiti in 1916 while working on *The Moon and Sixpence*. Although Maugham made his leading character an Englishman named Charles Strickland, the novel is based on Gauguin's life. Maugham found and purchased the glass doors Gauguin had

Book-inspired films
Clark Gable and Charles Laughton, who starred in the 1935 movie version of *Mutiny on the Bounty*, never came to Tahiti, but local villages provided the beautiful backgrounds. The 1962 remake with Marlon Brando, however, was filmed on Tahiti and Bora Bora. And Moorea provided the scenery for the *The Bounty*, a 1984 version featuring Mel Gibson and Anthony Hopkins.

The Hurricane, a novel by Mutiny authors Charles Nordhoff and James Norman Hall, was made into two films. One in 1937 starred Dorothy Lamour. A 1979 remake starring Mia Farrow was filmed on Bora Bora but bombed at the box office.

Based on his experiences in the Marquesas Islands, Herman Melville's novel, *Typee*, was filmed in 1958 as *Enchanted Island*, starring Jane Powell.

Herman Melville

Dirty dancing
'The young girls when ever they can collect eight or ten together dance a very indecent dance, which they call Timorodee singing most indecent songs and useing most indecent actions in the practice of which they are brought up from their earlyest Childhood.' – Capt James Cook, 1769.

painted for his Mataiea landlord *(see page 45)*. He also wrote a number of short stories about the Pacific, mostly compiled in *The Trembling of a Leaf*. One of these, 'The Fall of Edward Bernard', is a poignant tale of a young American who falls under the spell of Tahitian culture.

No work of literature added as much to Tahiti's fame as did *Mutiny on the Bounty*, penned in 1933 by Charles Nordhoff and James Norman Hall, the two young Americans who moved to Tahiti to write magazine articles. The novel became a huge bestseller and was made into three movie versions – in 1935, 1962 and most recently in 1984. Hall lived on Tahiti until his death in 1951, and his reconstructed home has been turned into a museum *(see page 34)*.

James A. Michener visited many of the islands in the South Pacific, including Bora Bora, while serving as a United States naval historian during World War II. Although his *Tales of the South Pacific* – which became the Broadway musical *South Pacific* – was set in the New Hebrides (now called Vanuatu), Michener later wrote *Return to Paradise* in 1950, which contains a short story set on Tahiti and an essay about the territory.

Traditonal dancer at the Tiki Theatre Village

TAHITIAN DANCE AND MUSIC

Of all the traditional customs, the most cherished in French Polynesia are its traditional dances. There are four different types of dances which are performed at important celebrations called *heiva*. You may see some of these performed at dinner shows at resort hotels, but the best and most spectacular performances take place each July at the Heiva i Tahiti festival *(see page 104)*.

Tahitian dance, like many other traditional Tahitian practices, was frowned upon by Christian missionaries, who deemed it suggestive and lewd. It carried on in secret, however, and is today experiencing a revival, thanks to dance companies who have succeeded in fusing traditional dance movements with modern choreography.

One of the most popular dances is the *otea* or war dance, originally a men-only dance but today performed by both sexes. *Aparima* is a graceful dance in which evocative hand movements spin a story in mime to the accompaniment of the ukelele or *himene* (hymn) singing. *Hivinau* is the simplest of Tahitian dances and mimics the actions of 18th-century white sailors hoisting anchor to the shouts of 'heave now'. Finally, there is *paoa*, a dance associated with the making of *tapa* fabric, which is derived from tree bark.

Dancing in the street, and (bottom) at a show

Less traditional is the dramatic fire dance, always performed by a man and Samoan in origin, and the *tamure*, a more recent but popular dance form that is recognised by its vigorous hip-swinging routine.

Accompanying the dancers usually is a small orchestra playing a variety of traditional percussion instruments, the *toere*, *faatete* and *pahu*, all made of hollowed out logs, as well as the *vivo*, a nose flute, and the *pu* or conch shell.

Festivals

Tahitians usually go all out to celebrate during a festival. Other than the three-week long Heiva i Tahiti, the July bash that dwarfs all others, the schedule of events changes from year to year, so check with the **Tahiti Tourisme** (tel: 505700, www.tahiti-tourisme.com). Following are the major events throughout the islands:

> **Celebrating with gusto**
> Nowhere is the Heiva i Tahiti festival celebrated with more gusto than on Bora Bora. Beginning at least a month ahead of time, the locals build a complex of thatch huts on the Vaitape waterfront. Appearing from a distance to be a traditional Polynesian village, these rustic carnival huts serve for weeks as handicraft stalls, restaurants, billiard parlours, shooting galleries and game arcades.

Festival musicians

JANUARY–MARCH

1 January: New Year's eve and day celebrated with drinking and much merry making.

January/February: Chinese New Year sees a parade, martial arts demonstrations, Chinese dances and calligraphy exhibitions. The exact date changes from year to year, depending on the Chinese lunar calendar.

February, second Saturday: Tahiti Nui Marathon is actually held on Moorea, where more than 600 participants run around the island, the biggest marathon on the islands.

5 March: Islanders celebrate the arrival of Protestant missionaries in 1797 by attending each other's church services, which are punctuated by hymn-singing and chanting.

APRIL–JUNE

May, first week: Professional surfers from all over the Pacific ride the mighty big waves in the Billabong Tahiti Pro Surfing Tournament at Teahupoo, on the south coast of Tahiti Iti.

June, first week: Amateurs and regional professionals play the Atimaono links during the Tahiti International Golf Open.

June, first 10 days: Private yachts sail among Huahine, Raiatea, Tahaa and Bora Bora during the Tahiti Nui Cup regatta.

29 June: Autonomy Day celebrates the granting of local governmental autonomy in 1984.

JULY–SEPTEMBER

June: Throughout this month, popular pageants are organised to pick the most beautiful 'Mr' and 'Miss' for each island.

July: During the first three weeks, Heiva i Tahiti (Festival of Tahiti) takes place on all the islands, with most of the big events held in Papeete. The festival began more than 115 years ago as the Bastille Day *fête* in celebration of the French national holiday on July 14.

Over the years it has expanded to include most of the month of July, and the name was changed to reflect its predominately Polynesian aspects. The most spectacular event is a countrywide dance competition held before an audience of thousands at Place Toata on the Papeete waterfront. Out on the harbour, both men and women compete for the national outrigger canoe racing championships.

Other competitions feature traditional Polynesian sports such as fire walking and coconut husking. In Pirae, an arts and crafts festival is the largest exposition of traditional and modern handicrafts.

Mid-August: Polynesian Artists Festival highlights local crafts on the Papeete waterfront.

Below: a song for all seasons
Bottom: outrigger canoe race

OCTOBER–DECEMBER

October, first Saturday: Competitors run, bike and swim around Moorea in the world's most beautiful *Aitoman* (Ironman) race.

October, third weekend: Outrigger canoes race among the Leeward Islands to compete for the Hawaiki Nui Va'a championship. This three-day canoe race is the most important sporting event in the calendar and attracts much hoopla.

October, third week: Tahiti Carnival features a parade and huge party on the Papeete waterfront.

1 November: Families whitewash tombstones and place flowers on graves on All Saints Day.

December, first week: Tiare Days see everyone wearing a *tiare Tahiti*, the national flower.

25 December: Christmas celebrations which stretches right into the New Year festivities.

FOOD AND DRINK

While Tahiti, Moorea and Bora Bora all have excellent Italian and Chinese restaurants, not surprisingly, classical French cuisine predominates in the territory, especially in the hotel and resort dining rooms.

The islands' chefs have ample fresh tuna, mahi-mahi and other deep sea fish on which to pour cream-laden sauces, plus shrimp farm-raised on Tahiti and Moorea and tender beef and lamb imported from New Zealand.

Indigenous Polynesian cuisine also makes an impression. Coconut milk is used in many preparations, including shrimp in a sweet sauce of blended curry and coconut cream, a popular dish on most restaurant menus. Creamy vanilla sauce is another mainstay.

The one local dish offered by even the most expensive restaurants is *poisson cru*; that is, raw tuna or mahi-mahi marinated in lime juice until 'cooked' and served with fresh onions, cucumbers, tomatoes and coconut milk.

French wine rules on the islands, with both *vin ordinaire* and fine vintages available. Beer drinkers will enjoy sipping a bottle of Hinano, the robust local brew.

Wine, beer and spirits are less expensive at *restaurants conentionneé*, which primarily cater to tourists and are thus entitled to a special licence that exempts them from the territory's high import tariff on alcoholic beverages.

TAHITIAN FEASTS

The Polynesians had no pots, pans, crockery, plates or utensils in ancient times. Instead, they cooked their meals in an *ahimaa* – a pit filled with heated stones. Suckling pig, fish, clams, taro

Opposite: fresh food in the fresh air

root and leaves, breadfruit, bananas and other tropical produce were well saturated with coconut milk and left to steam for hours.

After the food was cooked in these earth ovens, they would spread the meal on banana leaves and partake with their fingers. Dancing and music occupied the rest of the evening.

Many Tahitian families still prepare a traditional meal called a *tamaaraa*, with food cooked in an *ahimaa*, on Sundays, but visitors are most likely to experience such delicacies as part of Tahitian dance shows at the resorts. Guests pick their way along a buffet first, followed by a dance show on stage.

> **Money savers**
> In keeping with French custom, which favours lingering over a full meal accompanied by wine, many restaurants offer a *plat du jour* (plate of the day), particularly at midday. These usually feature fresh fish and vegetables bought at the market that morning. Another money saver: look out for special fixed-price 'tourist' menus at some of the more expensive restaurants. These three- or four-course meals offer fewer choices but are less expensive than regular menu offerings.

Restaurant Selection

Apart from Le Lotus in Tahiti, the restaurants recommended here are independent eateries found outside of hotels. They are listed according to these price categories: $$$ = expensive; $$ = moderate; $ = inexpensive.

Tahiti
Auberge du Pacifique, PK 11.2, Punaauia, tel: 439830. A fold-back roof lets starlight into this intimate lagoonside restaurant featuring a fine

blending of French and Polynesian cuisines. Owner Jean Galopin was a former chef at Maxims in Paris. A long-standing local favourite and highly recommended. Excellent wine list complements the food. $$$

Casablanca Cocktail Restaurant, Marina Taina, PK 9, Punaauia, tel: 439135. French and Moroccan cuisines are served at this dockside restaurant that features live jazz on Saturday evenings. Most dishes are expensive, but plain steaks and fish with chips are moderate options. $$$

Coco's, PK 13.5, Punaauia, tel: 582108. Located in the district of Punaauia, west of Papeete, French chef Philippe Baudet serves classic French cuisine with a Polynesian twist. Ask for a table in the garden if you prefer to dine *al fresco* and watch the sun setting over the peaks of Moorea, across the Sea of Moons, in the distance. $$$

Le Lotus, Inter-Continental Tahiti Beachcomber Resort, Faaa, tel: 865110, ext. 5512. The only hotel restaurant listed in this selection, visiting continental chefs here dish out the island's best cuisine in a romantic over-water dining room with gorgeous views of Moorea. An adjoining swim-ming pool with swim-up bar completes the picturesque lagoonside setting. $$$

Captain Bligh Restaurant and Bar, PK 11.4, Punaauia, tel: 436290. This huge lagoonside thatch-roof restaurant serves good if not extraordinary French and Polynesian fare. Traditional dance shows are featured on weekends, and a lagoonarium is part of the complex. $$

L'Api'zzeria, Blvd. Pomare, tel: 429830. Good pizza and a selection of pasta dishes served in a garden setting beside Papeete's main drag. $$

Le Belvédère, Fare Rau Ape Valley, tel: 427344. Swiss fondue (beef, seafood or cheese) is almost secondary to the simply awesome views from its location on a ridge high above Papeete. Wine and transportation are included in its fixed-price menu. The drive to the restaurant along a series of hairpin curves will surely whet appetites. $$

Le Rubis, Vaima Centre, rue Jeanne d'Arc, tel: 432555. A vineyard motif sets the scene for excellent French and Polynesian cuisine. Veteran chef prepares outstanding shrimp in coconut-curry sauce. $$

Les Trois Brasseurs, Blvd. Pomare, opposite Moorea ferry docks, tel: 506025. This restaurant and micro-brewery with four different kinds of

Le Retro in Papeete

home-brewed beer has outdoor sidewalk seating. Serves pub-style food and good sandwiches plus a daily lunch special. Limited English spoken. $$

Lou Pescadou, Rue Anne-Marie, behind Vaima Centre, tel: 437426. Papeete's best pizza and pasta served in cozy dining room trimmed with wine bottles and colourful murals of scenes from the Mediterranean. Friendly service. $$

Les roulottes

One of the least expensive ways to dine in French Polynesia is at *les roulottes*, portable meal wagons which set up shop on the local waterfronts. They are an institution in Papeete, where so many gather after dark at the cruise ship welcoming centre, on Boulevard Pomare at rue Gauguin, that they turn the scene into a veritable carnival.

Their most popular offerings are marinated raw fish, chargrilled steak and chicken served with chips (*steak frites* and *poulet frites*) and chow mein, chop suey and other simple Chinese dishes. But some also serve more sophisticated fare such as waffles (*gaufres*), crêpes, couscous and pizza.

Le Retro, Vaima Centre, Blvd. Pomare, tel: 428683. A Parisian-style sidewalk café that offers a wide variety of snacks as well as full meals. Or else sit back with a cappucino and watch the passing scene. $

L'Oasis du Vaima, Vaima Centre, Rue Général-de-Gaulle, tel: 454501. Serves wide selection of sandwiches, quiches, salads and ice-creams. Sit outdoors and watch Tahiti go by, or head upstairs for the air-conditioned restaurant which serves daily specials or *plat du jour*. $

Moorea

Les Nouveaux Mondes, Cook's Bay, tel: 564424. A large thatch roof provides tropical ambience for traditional French food, although local shrimp with coconut curry sauce is exceptional. Breakfast is served, too. $$$

Linareva Floating Restaurant and Bar, Haapiti, tel: 550566. Fine French-style seafood cooked and served in an old ferry boat. Seating is a bit cramped, but this is easily Moorea's best restaurant and widely acclaimed as such by local gourmands. $$$

Alfredo's, Pao Pao, tel: 561771. A converted grocery shop provides lively ambience for Italian and French fare. Very popular with American tourists seeking good value for money. Most of the dishes on the menu are good or better than average. Electic selection of jazz and Brazilian samba plays in the background while you dine. $$

Le Mahogany, Maharepa, tel: 563973. A long-time hotel chef presents very good French and Chinese cuisine. Moorea shrimp in whisky sauce is a speciality. Daily specials change frequently. A local favourite and known for its relaxed ambience. $$

Le Sud, Maharepa, tel: 564295. Proveçal, Spanish and Italian flavours offer a delicious break from traditional French fare at this small, intimate restaurant. $$

Restaurant Les Tipaniers, Hotel-Résidence Les Tipaniers, Haapiti, tel: 561267. Homemade pastas are bathed in both traditional and creative Italian sauces at this charming beachside thatch-roof restaurant. This is the best restaurant near Club Med. $$

The Blue Pineapple, Club Bali Hai, Cook's Bay, tel: 561206. Spectacular views accompany cooked-to-order breakfasts and lunches at the club's former waterside bar. $

Chez Capo, Haapiti, tel: 565489. This charmingly decorated and Tahitian-owned restaurant offers authentic

Island Nightlife

Papeete's lively nightlife scene is centred along the first block of rue des Ecoles, off Boulevard Pomare, which is home to several bars, clubs and discotheques. The gaudy neon signs come on at dark, but the action cranks up only after 9pm and goes until the wee hours, especially on Friday and Saturday.

This area also is the favourite haunt of the city's *mahu* (transvestite) community, who have made an institution of the **Le Piano Bar** (tel: 428824) and its late-night strip shows.

A mixed crowd frequents **Le Mana Rock Café** (tel: 483636) at rue des Ecoles, a three-storey club with both karaoke and a discotheque. Likewise too at the **Rolls Club** (tel: 434142) and **Le Tiffany's** (tel: 424001), two popular discos in the Vaima Centre on Boulevard Pomare.

On the quiet outer islands, visitors are most likely to spend their evenings at traditional Tahitian dance shows accompanied by a buffet of Polynesian food cooked in an earth oven. Every resort, including those on Tahiti, stages at least one Tahitian show and feast a week.

On Bora Bora, the **Club Med** (tel: 604604) often opens its doors for outsiders to dine, dance and watch its nightly musical revues.

Locals dance to island music on weekend nights at **Chez Billy Ruta** on Moorea (tel: 561254) and at **Le Récife Discothèque** (tel: 677387) on Bora Bora, but visitors beware: drunken fights can break out at these thoroughly unsophisticated institutions.

poisson cru (raw fish) and other local specialties. Breadfruit and taro accompany every meal. $

Le Sylesie Patisserie, Maharepa, tel: 561588. Breakfast and a wide variety of light meals at sidewalk tables next to the post office. $

Huahine

Eden Parc, Fitii, tel: 688658. Lush, often steamy gardens set the scene for fresh seafood accompanied by organically grown fruits and vegetables. Several vegetarian choices are available as well. Open for breakfast and lunch. $$

Snack Te Marara, Fare, tel: 687081. Tahitian specialties including excellent *poisson cru* as well as steak and fries and hamburgers are served on a covered deck beside the lagoon. A favourite among local residents. $$

Restaurant Tiare Tipanie, Fare, tel: 688052. Occupying the front porch of a private home, the restaurant serves the best – and only – pizza in town. $

Raiatea

Restaurant Quai des Pecheurs, Gare Maritime, Uturoa, tel: 664319. French country dishes are the highlight at this chic bistro, Raiatea's best all around restaurant. Tahitians play music and dance on weekend nights. $$

Seahorse, Gare Maritime, Uturoa, tel: 661634. Excellent Chinese fare served in a sophisticated setting beside the cruise ship dock. Weekends feature traditional Tahitian-style roast pork cooked in creamy coconut milk. $$

Brasserie Maraamu, Gare Maritime, Uturoa, tel: 664664. Plain but good local food includes fried chicken or steak with chips, marinated raw fish, Chinese stir-fries and other tasty dishes. Open for breakfast as well. $

Snack Moemoea, Waterfront, Uturoa, tel: 663984. Inside and sidewalk seating for the best hamburgers and marinated raw fish on Raiatea, plus sandwiches and steaks. Open for breakfast and lunch daily except Saturday afternoons and on Sundays. $

Tahaa

Chez Louise, Tiva, tel: 656888. Tahitian-style crab, lobster, shrimp and other seafood dishes predominate at this locally owned restaurant on Tahaa's west coast. On Wednesdays, a traditional *ahimaa* lunch is served. $$

Marina Iti, Apu Bay, tel: 656106. This small pension on the southern tip of the island offers Tahaa's best French fare. Reservations are required. $$

Bora Bora

Bamboo House, Matira, tel: 677624. A small rustic building built of bamboo and coconut logs sets the scene for good French-style seafood. $$$

Bloody Mary's Restaurant & Bar, Matira, tel: 677286. An attraction in itself, this famous restaurant with sand floor and coconut-log seats provides American-style chargrilled fish, shrimp and lobster as well as steak and chicken to a predominantly Yankee clientele. Make sure that you book in advance; it's said that dinner reservations are rationed among the hotels and cruise ships. $$$

Top Dive Restaurant, Vaitape, tel: 605050. A towering thatch roof, romantic lighting, lagoonside setting, and of course excellent French cuisine emphasizing seafood easily make this the best fine dining spot on all of Bora Bora. $$$

La Bounty, Matira, tel: 677043. Bora Bora's best pizza served here plus other reasonably priced French and Italian selections. Within walking distance of most Matira resorts. $$

Les snacks

Tahiti has McDonald's and Kentucky Fried Chicken outlets, but Tahitians much prefer to buy their fast food at a *les snack*, one of the multitude of snack bars that dot the islands. Most *les snacks* serve hamburgers and pizza, and all offer *casse-croûtes* – inexpensive sandwiches made from crusty French bread.

Matira Bar and Restaurant, Matira, tel: 677051. Quite ordinary Chinese and some French dishes but a gorgeous setting over Matira Beach. Sunsets from the terrace are quite stunning. $$

L'Appetisserie, Centre Commercial le Pahia, Vaitape, tel: 677888. Noted pastry chef provides the best breakfasts and lunchtime *plat du jour* on the island. Scrumptious cakes and pastries will satisfy most sweet tooths. $

Rangiroa

Vaimario Restaurant Pizzeria, main road west of airport, tel: 960469. Pizzas reign supreme at this small restaurant with verandah seating, plus meals featuring fish fresh from the lagoon simply grilled or smothered with traditional French sauces. $$

Barbecue favourite

SHOPPING

Many visitors spend their days hunting down that perfect black pearl, easily French Polynesia's most popular shopping item. Apart from that, a wide array of handicrafts, souvenirs, fabrics and tropical clothing like T-shirts and *pareu* (sarong) are available on all the main tourist islands. However, not all items are locally made, so if you want something authentic – and are willing to pay for it – make sure you see a label saying 'Made in Tahiti'.

BLACK PEARLS

Pearl farmers in the Tuamotu and Gambier islands produce so many pearls that these loose and set orbs seem to be for sale everywhere on the islands – touts even offer loose ones at the municipal markets. Overproduction has resulted in many low-quality pearls, however, so caution is advised if you decide to buy.

Cultured black pearls are produced when *pinctada margaritifera* oysters coat foreign substances – in this case a small, hand-inserted nucleus of oyster shell – with a lustrous substance known as nacre, which also constitutes mother-of-pearl.

While the nacre of other pearl species is white, the *pinctada margaritifera*'s ranges in colour from light grey to black laced with shades of other colours. The bulk of French Polynesia's crop is black with blue and brown tints. Most valuable are dark black pearls with peacock-like shades of rose and green showing through a rich lustre.

Size, shape and a lack of imperfections also determine the value of a pearl. The prices normally increase with size – most range from 10mm to 17mm in diameter – but smaller, perfectly symmetrical orbs or pear and tear-drop shaped pearls can be sometimes be more valuable than larger ones.

Most pearls have blemishes and some pitting; the less they have, the more valuable they are. Using the criteria explained, pearls are graded Gem, A, B, C or D quality. A Gem quality pearl, needless to say, is very rare and expensive.

There are numerous pearl merchants in Tahiti, but before you begin your pearl hunt, be sure to pay a visit to the **Musée de la Perle Robert Wan**, in Papeete's Vaima Centre (tel: 454345, Mon to Sat 9.30am–noon and 1–7pm), which explains how pearls are grown, harvested, graded and brought to the market. The museum's description of how pearls are valued is interesting even if you are not planning to buy any pearls.

Large, country-wide merchants such as **Tahiti Perles**, **South Sea Pearls** and **Sibani Perles** have shops on Tahiti and the other main islands and in many resorts. Their relatively expensive selections are generally of very high quality. The **Vaima Centre** in Tahiti is a good place to shop as most of the big retailers have outlets there. **Ron Hall's Island Fashion Black Pearls** on Moorea (tel: 561106) and **Matira Pearls** on Bora Bora (tel: 677914), both owned by Americans, offer a wide range of prices and quality.

> **Shopping in Papeete**
> Small boutiques on all the main tourist islands carry handicrafts, souvenirs and clothing, but the widest selection and best prices are found on the second level of Papeete's bustling Marché Municipale (Mon to Fri 5am–6pm, Sat 5am–1pm Sun 5–8am; *see also page 54*).

HANDICRAFTS AND FABRICS

The locals also produce a wide range of handicrafts, from wooden bowls and straw baskets to shell necklaces and intricate applique cotton quilts known as *tifaifai*. Missionary women from New England in the United States taught the local women how to make the colourful patchwork quilts in the early 19th century, and the art has survived to the present, albeit with the help of sewing machines.

Indigeneous *tapa* fabrics, made by pounding the bark of the paper mulberry tree into thin sheets is difficult to come by and is only produced by the women on Fatu Hiva island in the remote Marquesas group.

One of the easiest souvenirs to take home is a colourful *pareu*, or sarong, which Tahitians wear at home and everyone uses at the beach. Gaudy tie-dyed models are plentiful and inexpensive, especially at Papeete's Marché Municipale in Tahiti. Artistic hand-painted *pareu* cost more but make fine wall hangings.

SCULPTURE

The Tahitians were noted wood and stone carvers in pre-European times. Most *marae* – pre-Christian temples made of coral or basaltic stone – were adorned with intricately carved *tiki*

Marvellous monoi

Monoi, a rich and fragrant emollient made of a blend of coconut oil and dried herbs and flowers was traditionally used by the Polynesians to moisturise their bronzed skins and slick down their black hair. These days, *monoi* is used in a variety of cosmetic products like soap, shampoo, bath gels, body lotion and sunscreens.

figurines. The Polynesians believed that their gods would reside temporarily in these stone or wooden *tiki* during religious ceremonies.

When the Protestant missionaries arrived at the end of the 18th century, they considered the *tiki* to be idols and ordered them all destroyed in the Society Islands. Only the Marquesas and Austral island groups escaped the ban, and today wood carvings from the Marquesas are among the best handicrafts available.

Since the time of Gauguin, European artists have always been drawn by the colours and light of French Polynesia. Galleries in Papeete display the work of a number of foreign and local artists. Cheaper prints and posters are also available.

Shopping for pearls

ACTIVE HOLIDAYS

Rare is the beachside resort hotel that does not have a scuba diving base plus canoes, windsurfing boards, sailboats, snorkelling gear and other equipment for its guests' use. Barrier reefs create calm, clear, warm lagoons everywhere in French Polynesia, perfect for a variety of watersports.

Less strenuous are dolphin-watching excursions, swimming off the resort beach, and '*motu* picnics' which combine boating, snorkelling, fishing and lunch on a deserted *motu* (islet) out on the reef. A comprehensive list of waterports activities and operators in the various islands are found at www.tahitisun.com.

DIVING AND SNORKELLING

Most lagoons are well stocked with a plethora of bright tropical fish, which helps to compensate for coral reefs bleached almost white by warm seawater brought by the recent El Niño climatic phenomenon. This means that French Polynesia is a better spot for divers and snorkellers to observe fish than to see colourful coral.

Diving and snorkelling are good everywhere, but marine life is most plentiful in the lagoons of the Tuamotu Islands – Rangiroa, Manihi and Tikehau. Rangiroa is famous for its plentiful sharks and manta rays, while Manihi and Tikehau have greater varieties of fish. Divers and snorkellers can take heart-stopping rides on the rip tide through the passes leading into the lagoons of Rangiroa and Manihi *(see pages 90 and 94)*.

There are more than 30 dive centres on Tahiti, Moorea, Raiatea, Tahaa, Huahine and Bora Bora in the Soceity Islands as well as in the Tuamotu Islands of Rangiroa, Manihi and Tikehau. More remote are dive schools on

> ### 👁 Feeding the sharks
> Shark-feeding adds an excitement to diving excursions on Moorea, Huahine and Bora Bora. While a guide feeds reef sharks into a frenzy, guests watch – from a safe underwater distance. Shark-feeding has been criticised roundly by environmentalists, and some say it accounts for the recent spate of shark attacks on humans around the world. But due to its popularity in Tahiti, it shows no signs of abatement.

Nuka Hiva in the Marquesas Islands and on Rurutu and Tubuai in the Austral Islands.

Both resort-based diving and more expensive live-aboard dive trips are available. For more information, visit www.diving-tahiti.com.

SURFING

Surfers of all capabilities can ride the waves breaking on Tahiti's black sand beaches. Prime spots for surf breaks are found at Papenoo, Paea and Papara, and the Punaauia and Taapuna passes, but the best boarding experience is experienced on Huahine's reefs – not an adventure for the novice or the faint-of-heart. In Tahiti, **Moana Surf Tours** (tel: 437070) and **Tura I Mataare Surf School** (tel: 454400) are well known.

FISHING

Game fishing is available all year round in French Polynesia and charter boats from all the main islands go in search of fish like blue marlin, mahimahi, tuna, wahoo and other deep-sea fish. **Tahiti Sporting and Adventure** (tel: 410225/7; fax: 452758) in Punaaina, Tahiti, is a reputable booking agent for fishing boats.

YACHT CHARTERING

Enclosed by a single barrier reef, Raiatea and Tahaa are two of the world's most beautiful places to charter a yacht. Tahaa can be circumnavigated without leaving the protection of the reef, and both islands have numerous quiet anchorages in mountain-fringed bays. More adventurous sailors can cross the open sea to Huahine and Bora Bora, both within sight of Raiatea and Tahaa. **The Moorings** (tel: 663593, fax: 662094, www.moorings.com) and **Sunsail Yacht Charters** (tel: 662318, fax: 662319, www.sunsail.com) have bases on Raiatea.

GOLF

Atimaono Golf Course (tel: 574032) has the territory's only links. The 18-hole, 6,950-yard course is 40km (25 miles) from Papeete on Tahiti's south coast. Equipment rentals are available and the clubhouse has a restaurant and a swimming pool.

CYCLING

The mostly sealed round-islands roads are relatively flat, making for good bicycling for even out-of-shape riders. Some of the highland trails attract mountain bikers, but these are not marked and guides are necessary *(see 'Walking' this page)*. Except on Tahiti, car rental agencies rent bicycles as well, and many resorts provide them for their guests' use.

WALKING

Anyone will enjoy walking along the coastal roads, with mountains on one side and blue lagoons on the other. Tahiti, Moorea, and Bora Bora also have a network of mountain trails, including one across Tahiti and another up a breathtaking ridge spine to its highest mountaintop.

The trails are not marked, however, so local guides are absolutely essential (contact the tourist office). Also essential: drinking water, rain gear and jackets – it rains almost daily up in the mountains, and despite the tropical latitude, it can get cold at high altitudes.

HORSE RIDING

Small ranches provide horse rides along the beaches and into the mountainous interiors of Tahiti, Moorea, Huahine and Raiatea. On Huahine, **La Petite Ferme** (tel and fax: 688298) also has two- and three-day combined riding and camping excursions. On Tahiti, **Ranch Gauguin** (tel: 575100) takes you on winding trails through the valleys of the southern coast.

Surfing is not for the faint-hearted

PRACTICAL INFORMATION

Getting There

By Air

Although cruise ships occasionally stop in French Polynesia on trans-Pacific voyages, air is the only practical way to get to Tahiti. Tahiti-Faaa International Airport, 7km (4 miles) from downtown Papeete on the northwest corner of Tahiti, is the territory's sole international airport. At least one flight a day arrives from Los Angeles, less frequently from Paris, Auckland, Sydney, Oakland (California), Honolulu, Japan, Fiji and Chile.

Carriers that serve Tahiti include:
Air New Zealand: www.airnz.com
Air France: www.airfrance.com
Air Tahiti Nui: www.airtahiti-nui.com
Hawaiian Airlines: www.hawaiianair.com
LanChile Airlines: www.lanchile.com
Qantas Airways: www.qantas.com

Getting Around

By Air

Flying is the most dependable way to get between the islands. Air Moorea (tel: 864141, fax: 864299) shuttles small planes between Tahiti and Moorea, a 7-minute flight each way. Air Tahiti (tel: 864242, fax: 864069, www.airtahiti.pf) provides reliable scheduled service between Tahiti and the other islands, with several flights a day to Bora Bora, and at least daily to Huahine, Raiatea, Rangiroa and Manihi. Air Tahiti offers discounted multi-island fares on popular tourist routes. Wan Air (tel: 855554, fax: 855556, www.wanair.pf) also flies between Tahiti, Raiatea, Rangiroa and Bora Bora.

Seats on all three airlines can be purchased as part of your overseas ticket. With a few exceptions, flights operate only during daylight hours. Passengers connecting to or from international flights within seven days may check up to 20kg (44 pounds) of luggage on domestic flights; otherwise the limit is 10kg (22 pounds).

> **Sit on the 'right' side**
> For the best views of the islands, sit on the left side of the plane flying from Tahiti, and on the right side coming back.

By Ferry

The fast catamarans *Aremiti* (tel: 505757) and *Moorea Explorer* (tel: 868747) operate ferry services daily between Papeete and Vaiare on Moorea's east coast. Both make at least two return trips in the early morning, one about midday, and two in the late afternoon. Buses meet the morning and late afternoon ferries on Moorea but not those arriving at midday. Reservations are not accepted.

Another fast catamaran, the *Aremiti III* (tel: 428585), makes two weekly voyages from Papeete to Huahine, Raiatea, Tahaa and Bora Bora, as do the slower passenger-and-vehicle ferries *Vaeanu* (tel: 412535) and *Hawaiki Nui* (tel: 452324). They usually depart Papeete at nightfall and arrive at Huahine during the night.

By Cruise Ship

Three large cruise ships based in Papeete take passengers to various islands on voyages ranging from seven to 17 days.

Most unusual is the *Aranui III* (tel: 426240, fax: 434889, www.aranui.com), a working cargo vessel with air-conditioned berths for 200 passengers on 17-day voyages from Tahiti to the Tuamotu and Marquesas islands. Experts on history and archaeology come along to lead passengers on dry-land excursions while the ship is loading cargo at its island stopovers.

Most luxurious is Radisson Seven Seas Cruises' 320-passenger *Paul Gauguin* (tel: 545100, www.rssc.com), which makes one-week circuits from Tahiti to Moorea, Huahine, Raiatea and Bora Bora. It has a stern platform from which passengers can take part in watersports without going ashore.

Largest and least expensive of the ships is the 700-passenger *Tahitian Princess* (tel: 425561, www.princesscruises. com), which usually makes 10-day voyages through the Society Islands. Its sister ship, the *Pacific Princess*, operates in French Polynesia during part of the year.

Based at Raiatea, the smaller and more intimate *Tu Moana* and *Tia Moana* (tel: 451066, www.boraboracruises. com) each carries up to 74 passengers on one-week cruises through the Leeward Islands. Unlike the larger vessels, these ships can anchor close to shore, thus affording passengers a chance to breakfast while sitting at tables resting in the shallow lagoon.

Except for short voyages between islands, the ships spend their time anchored in the lagoon or tied to a wharf at each island.

BY CAR AND SCOOTER

With public transportation confined primarily to Tahiti, rental cars and scooters are the best ways to get around the islands. Each island has one main road, usually running along the narrow plains and skirting their lagoons, so getting lost is almost impossible.

The price of petrol is roughly comparable with that in the UK. Petrol stations are plentiful in Papeete and its suburbs, less so in the rural areas and on the other islands.

Drivers must bring their valid national drivers' licences (an international licence is not necessary).

The main traffic regulations are as follows: driving is on the right-hand side of the road, seat belts must be worn, helmets are required on scooters, and drivers must stop for pedestrians at marked crosswalks.

Vehicles on the main roads have the right-of-way, but in Papeete they must give way to others entering from the right unless the intersection is marked by a traffic signal.

Speed limits are 60kmph (36mph) to 110kmph (66mph) on the Rte 5 motorway on Tahiti, 80kmph (48mph) on all other rural roads, and 40kmph (24mph) in towns and villages.

Tahiti has one of the highest per capita highway accident death rates in the world, so drivers should always be alert and drive defensively.

Hiring a Car or Scooter

Avis (tel: 419393, www.avis.com), Hertz (tel: 420472, www.hertz.com) and Europcar (tel: 452424, www.europcar.com) have agencies on the major islands. Scooters are available on the outer islands but not on Tahiti. Shortage of rental vehicles occur whenever cruise ships are in port, and on weekends on Moorea, so book far in advance. Drivers must be at least 25 years of age and have a major credit card.

BY BUS

Only Tahiti has public buses. The famous *le truck* – colourful wooden passenger compartments built on flatbed trucks – are the most economical form of transport between the Papeete waterfront and the west coast hotel district (daily 6am–10.30pm), but they are a thing of the past elsewhere on the island, where they have been replaced by modern – but not air conditioned – buses. *Le truck* and buses fan out from Papeete along the east and west coasts of Tahiti, but none travels completely around the island.

'Safari' tours
Every hotel activities desk offers sightseeing tours by air-conditioned bus, and those on Tahiti, Moorea, Huahine, Raiatea and Bora Bora will also book excursions by open-air, four-wheel drive vehicles. The leisurely guided bus tours usually follow the round-island roads, with stops at the major sights along the way, but the more adventurous 'safari' tours bump their way over dirt tracks to plantations and spectacular overlooks in the mountainous interiors. The tours range in price from XFP 3,500 to XFP 5,000 (US$26–$37.50) for half a day, and XFP 5,500 to XFP 7,500 (US$41–$56) for all day.

BY TAXI

Taxis are plentiful only on Tahiti, and they are relatively expensive everywhere, especially after dark when fares more than double. Although the government sets the fares (they are posted in the arrivals concourse at Tahiti-Faaa International Airport and on Boulevard Pomare outside the Vaima Centre in Papeete), it's advisable to agree on the fare with the driver before setting out.

Hotels generally are not permitted to pick up their guests at the airports on Tahiti and Moorea, so travellers not met there by a tour operator must take taxis to their accommodations. However, hotels can pick up guests on the other islands.

Facts for the Visitor

TRAVEL DOCUMENTS

All visitors except French nationals must have a valid passport, and everyone except citizens of European Union countries must possess a return air ticket. Citizens of the EU nations as well as Switzerland and Australia do not require a visa for visits of up to three months. Citizens of most other European countries, the US, Canada, New Zealand, Singapore, Chile and several other countries may stay for one month without a visa.

Applications can be made at the immigration office at Tahiti-Faaa International Airport to extend the initial one-month visa for up to two more months. Citizens of most other nations must get a visa stamped 'Valid for French Polynesia' from the French embassy or consulate in their respective home countries.

For a complete list of visa requirements for various nationals, look up the website of the Tahiti Tourisme *(see below)*. Vaccinations are not required unless you're arriving from an infected area.

Customs

Duty-free allowances are 200 cigarettes or 50 cigars, two litres of spirits or wine and 50 grams of perfume. Narcotics, dangerous drugs, weapons, ammunition and all live animals including pets are prohibited.

TOURIST INFORMATION

The territory's official tourism promotion office, Tahiti Tourisme, BP 65, Papeete, tel: 505700, fax: 436619; www.tahiti-tourisme.com; or e-mail: tahititourisme@mail.pf, will supply information to help plan your holiday before you leave home. Tahiti Tourisme has the following overseas offices:

UK: c/o BGB & Associates, 7 Westminster Palace Gardens, Artillery Row, London SW, IP IRL, tel: (44 20) 7233-2300; fax: 7233-2301, e-mail: virginia@bgb.co.uk.

North America: 300 N. Continental Blvd., Suite 160, El Segundo, CA 90245, tel: (310) 414-8484, fax: 414-8490, www.gototahiti.com.

Australia: 12 Ann Street, Surry Hills, NSW 2010, tel: (612 2) 9281-6020, fax: 9211-6589), www.traveltotahiti.com.au.

USEFUL WEBSITES

In addition to Tahiti Tourisme's website, here are a few others with useful information on French Polynesia. www.polynesianislands.com/fp: Covers other South Pacific islands in addition to French Polynesia.

www.pacifictravel.com.au: Australia-based website providing coverage of all the South Pacific islands.

www.tahiti.com: California-based commercial site with background information as well as chat rooms, tourism updates and news on discount packages.

www.tahiti-explorer.com: A travel agency site with chat room and extensive reports on recent trips written by its clients.

www.tahiti-guide.com: Tahiti Resort Guide, a travel club, sponsors this site with photos showing 360° views of many resort hotel rooms and bungalows.

www.tahiti-nui.com: Tahiti's largest travel agency's site has background information and booking facilities for hotels, domestic transportation and package tours.

www.tahitisun.com: California-based commercial site with chat rooms and a wealth of background information posted on separate websites dedicated to each island: www.papeete.com, www.mooreaisland.com, www.boraboraisland.com, www.huahineisland.com, www.raiatea.com, www.manihi.com and www.teitaroa.com.

> **Live 'weathercam'**
> Click on the webcam icon of Tahiti Nui Travels' website: www.tahiti-nui.com to see a live shot of Papeete harbour. This will give you a good indication of the current weather in Tahiti.

CURRENCY AND EXCHANGE

The French Pacific Franc (XFP) is the official currency. Locally, it is known as CFP (Colonial Pacific Franc). Notes come in denominations of 500, 1,000, 5,000, 10,000 and 50,000 francs; coins in 1, 2, 5, 10, 20, 50 and 100 francs. The XFP is tied directly to the European Euro at an exchange rate of 1 Euro = 119.33 XFP. At time of going to press, US$1 was roughly equivalent to 100 XFP.

The easiest way to obtain cash on the main islands is with a MasterCard or Visa credit or debit card at a bank ATM machine (which are non-existent in the Tuamotu Islands). All banks will exchange foreign currency and travellers' cheques, but will charge up to 500 XFP commission per transaction. Exchange rates vary little from one bank to another.

American Express, Diner's Club,

Cruise ship in Raiatea

MasterCard and Visa cards are accepted by most hotels and car-rental firms, but most restaurants and shops will take only MasterCard and Visa.

TIPPING

Tipping is officially frowned upon as being against the Polynesian tradition of hospitality and is not expected, although the custom has made inroads at restaurants in the prime tourist areas.

OPENING TIMES

Most shops are open 7.30–11.30am and 1.30–5pm Monday to Friday and 7.30–11.30am Saturday, although a few remain open through the lunch period and some until 8pm. Most village grocery shops also open 2–6pm on Saturday and 6–8am on Sunday.

Although they vary slightly from branch to branch, banking hours generally are 8–11.45am and 1.30–3pm Monday to Thursday, and 8–11.45am and 1.30–4pm on Friday.

PUBLIC HOLIDAYS

Government offices and most shops/businesses close on New Year's Day (January 1), Missionary Day (March 5), Good Friday and Easter Monday (March/April), Ascension Day (40 days after Easter), Whitmonday (seventh Monday after Easter), Labour Day (May 1), Pentecost Monday (first Monday in June), National Day (July 14), Assumption Day (August 15), Internal Autonomy Day (September 8), All Saints Day (November 1), Armistice Day (November 11), and Christmas Day (December 25).

POSTAL SERVICES

Every town and main village has a post office, which also doubles as the telecommunications centre. Hours vary slightly, but most are open from 7am–3pm Monday to Friday, 8–11am Saturday.

TELEPHONES

The country code for French Polynesia is 689. There are no local area codes, so from overseas dial your country's international access number followed by 689 and the six-digit phone number.

All public phones require a phone card (*télécarte*), available at all post offices and most grocery shops.

Overseas calls can be placed at any post office, although the easiest and least expensive way to call home is from a public phone. The 24-hour rate for direct-dialled overseas calls is 100 XFP per minute.

Mobile phones operate on the GSM 900 network. Vini, tel: 481313, a branch of the post and telecommunications bureau, operates the local service and rents mobile phones. Note that most American mobile phones will not work in French Polynesia.

ELECTRICITY

Electrical power is 220 volts, 50 cycles. Plugs are two-prong, so a continental adapter is essential for visitors from Britain, the US, Canada, Australia and New Zealand. Most hotels have 110-volt outlets for shavers.

TIME

French Polynesia is 10 hours behind Greenwich Mean Time. There is no summer or daylight savings time.

Logging on

The major islands have at least one cyber café providing Internet access. If you brought your laptop and use Windows, you can set up a new dial-up connection in My Computer. Enter the phone number as 36888 and both your user name and password as ANONYMOUS (in all capital letters). The cost of each connection will be billed directly to your hotel room.

MEDICAL ASSISTANCE

Every town and village has a public hospital, and many also have private clinics. Most doctors are trained in France, and health care is of a reasonably high standard.

In case of a medical emergency, you should go to the emergency department of the nearest hospital or clinic, or dial 17. In Papeete, both Clinic Paofai, on Boulevard Pomare, tel: 437700 and Clinque Cardella, on rue Anne-Marie-Javouhey, tel: 428010, are open 24 hours.

Although local residents are entitled to free health care at the public hospitals, all visitors must pay for treatment and are advised to take out accident and illness insurance coverage.

A green cross on a white background is the symbol for a chemist. Most are well stocked primarily with French products. Pharmacies rotate night duty in Papeete; ask your hotel desk staff which one is open after dark. Pharmacists can be contacted for emergency service on the outer islands. Check with your resort.

EMERGENCIES

For police, fire and ambulance, tel: 17. French national *gendarme* police the entire territory and have the power to arrest. Municipal police enforce traffic regulations but cannot arrest suspected criminals. *Gendarmes* and local police officers rarely speak English.

CLOTHING

The tropical climate dictates summertime clothing all year-round, although a sweater or windcheater will be useful if travelling in the mountains anytime or after dark during the cooler, windier months from June to September. Shorts are acceptable everywhere except at church and a few expensive restaurants. Local men tend to wear slacks and colourful tropical shirts, and women put on long skirts, when going out at night. Beach wear can be as brief as you like; in fact, women can swim and sunbathe topless at the beaches.

ETIQUETTE

Most Tahitians tend to be shy but warm quickly to strangers who extend a friendly smile. They also have a sense of propriety despite their reputation for sexual largesse, so do not offend them by engaging in activities that would not be permitted at home.

PHOTOGRAPHY

These gorgeous islands are a photographer's feast, so bring your camera or camcorder along. Colour print film is widely available, and one-hour processing is available in Papeete. Both are slightly more expensive than at home. Camcorder cassettes, camera batteries and colour slide film are not as readily available, so bring enough to see you through.

THEFT

Street crime is not a serious problem in the islands, but property theft is. Do not leave valuables unattended anywhere. Take all the usual precautions to prevent car break-ins and theft, particularly in the main tourist centres. Never leave anything of value in your hotel room (use the hotel safe) or rental car (keep the doors and boot locked). Notify the police immediately if you are the victim of theft, as your insurance company will need written confirmation when you submit a claim.

Unless you know you will need your passport, leave it in the hotel safe and carry a photocopy of the identification page.

DIPLOMATIC REPRESENTATION

There are no embassies or consulate offices in French Polynesia.

ACCOMMODATION

With official government policy favouring high-end properties, most accommodation comprises mainly expensive (20,000 XFP and up) beach-side resorts. Moderately priced (10,000–20,000 XFP) and inexpensive (under 10,000 XFP) accommodation is limited throughout the territory.

The government does not assign a rating system to the hotels and resorts but does maintain a list of 'unclassified' hotels and pensions *(see panel below)*.

HOTELS AND RESORTS

With a few exceptions, primarily on Tahiti where traditional hotels predominate, the expensive resorts consist of thatch-roof guest bungalows grouped around a central building housing the restaurant, bar, activities desk and shops. Most but not all have over-water bungalows *(see page 125)* and swimming pools.

Most resorts offer optional meal packages. It is recommended that these be purchased on Rangiroa, which has few restaurants outside the resorts, and especially on Manihi, which has none at all.

> ⚡ **'Unclassified' pensions**
> Although there are no traditional bed-and-breakfast inns or guest houses in the territory, Tahiti Tourisme maintains a list of 'unclassified' pensions and small hotels.
>
> Most pensions are operated by Tahitian families who provide a simple bedroom, a bathroom (often shared with the family) and a tropical breakfast. If you go this route, a working knowledge of French will be most helpful.
>
> For more information contact Tahiti Tourisme, BP 65, Papeete, tel: 505700, fax: 436619, www.tahiti-tourisme.com; e-mail: tahiti-tourisme@mail.pf.

HOSTELS

Although there are no official youth hostels in French Polynesia, Moorea, Huahine and Bora Bora have inexpensive establishments catering to backpackers. Most provide campsites, simple bungalows or rooms, and communal kitchens, showers and toilets. Very few provide hot-water showers.

Hotel Selection

These suggestions for hotels in French Polynesia are listed according to the following categories: $$$ = expensive; $$=moderate; $=inexpensive.

Tahiti

Inter-Continental Tahiti Beachcomber Resort, BP 6014, Faaa, Tahiti, www.interconti.com, tel: 865110, fax: 865130. Located on the northwest corner of the island, Tahiti's top resort lacks a natural beach but every room has a view of Moorea. Units range from standard to luxurious hotel rooms plus over-water bungalows located on a private island and linked to the hotel by a bridge. Le Lotus restaurant is considered the island's best *(see page 108)*. $$$

Le Meridien Tahiti, BP 380595, Tamanu, tel: 470707, fax: 470708, www.lemeridien-tahiti.com. Balinese-style main buildings highlight this resort beside one of the few white sand beaches on Tahiti, 8km (5 miles) south of the airport. Spacious rooms are luxurious but only over-water bungalows have views of Moorea. Traffic congestion however can mean a slow trip to/from airport during rush hour. $$$

Radisson Plaza Resort Tahiti, BP 14170, Arue, tel: 488888, fax: 835513, www.radisson.com). This 165-unit luxury hotel (which opened in August 2004) sits beside the black sands of Lafayette Beach, 7km (4 miles) east of downtown Papeete. Most expensive units are townhouse-style, with upstairs bedrooms and bathrooms. $$$

Sheraton Hotel Tahiti, BP 416, Papeete, tel: 864848, fax: 864840, www.sheraton.com. This lagoonside hotel is conveniently located to both the Papeete waterfront and the airport. Well-appointed rooms have water views, some of Moorea. Its sand-bottomed 2,000 sq m (6,561 sq ft) pool compensates for a lack of beach $$$

Sofitel Maeva Beach, BP 6008, Papeete, Tahiti, tel: 428042, fax: 438470, www.accorhotels.com. An older hotel near the Inter-Continental Tahiti Beachcomber that remains in need of renovation. Has smaller rooms than its neighbour but is less expensive. $$$

Le Royal Tahitien Hotel, BP 5001, Pirae, Tahiti, tel: 504040, fax: 504041, www.royaltahitien.com. Lush gardens beside a black-sand beach distinguish this good-value hotel in a residential suburb 4km (2½ miles) east of downtown Papeete. Beachside restaurant offering good French fare has nice Tahit-

ian ambience; other buildings however are more Scandinavian than Polynesian in style. $$

Hotel Tiare Tahiti, BP 2359, Papeete, tel: 500100, fax: 436847, e-mail: hotel tiaritahiti@mail.pf. This five-storey hotel is the least expensive hotel in town, but its location on Boulevard Pomare can send traffic noise into its rather spartan rooms. Breakfast is included in the room rate but the hotel offers few other amenities. $$

Moorea

Inter-Continental Moorea Beachcomber Resort, BP 1019, Papetoai, Moorea, tel: 551919, fax: 551955, www.interconti.com. Between Papetoai village and the Club Med, the former Moorea Beachcomber Parkroyal has the island's widest array of watersports, including dolphin-watching, plus Moorea's only children's programme. Accommodations range from hotel rooms to over-water bungalows. $$$

Sheraton Moorea Lagoon Resort & Spa, BP 416, Papeete, tel: 864848, fax:

Poolside, Sofitel Maeva Beach

864840, www.sheraton.com. Relatively isolated between Cook's and Opunohu bays, one of Moorea's most luxurious resort boasts the island's best amenities and a full-service spa. Many of the identical bungalows are perched over water. $$$

Sofitel Ia Ora, BP 28, Maharepa, Moorea, tel: 550355 or 410404 in Papeete, fax: 410505, www.accorhotels.com. Older all-bungalow resort on the east coast is isolated from restaurants and activities; needs to improve service and prevent insects from entering the rooms. However, makes up for it with Moorea's best beach and a most colourful lagoon, plus unparalleled views of Tahiti. $$$

Club Bali Hai Moorea, BP 8, Maharepa, tel: 561368, fax: 561327, www.clubbalihai.com. A partial time-share operation, this older hotel in Paopao has the least expensive over-water bungalows in French Polynesia plus a few inexpensive hotel rooms. Its lovely Blue Pineapple restaurant *(page 109)* has phenomenal views of Cook's Bay. $$

Moorea Pearl Resort & Spa, BP 3410, Maharepa, tel: 551750, fax: 551751, www.pearlresorts.com. Replacing the famous Hotel Bali Hai in 2002, this resort has a variety of accommodation ranging from hotel rooms to over-water bungalows. Large outdoor pool is more attractive than the beach, but the snorkelling offshore is very good. Wide range of amenities, including a full-service spa. $$

Hotel-Résidence Les Tipaniers, BP 1002, Papetoai, tel: 561267, fax: 562925, www.lestipaniers.com. Small, friendly hotel shares beach with Club Med. Recently refurbished bungalows are clean and comfortable. Motel rooms are least expensive accommodations on Moorea. The excellent Les Tipaniers Italian restaurant adjoins *(see page 109)* the hotel. $$

Hotel Kaveka, BP 373, Maharepa, tel: 565050, fax: 565263, www.hotelkaveka.com. A basic, all-bungalow hotel, this bayside choice is favoured by budget-conscious package tourists. Spectacular Cook's Bay views are better than the food in its over-water restaurant. $

Huahine

Sofitel Heiva, BP 38, Fare, tel: 688586 or 410404 in Papeete, fax: 410505, www.accorhotels.com. Located at the end of Motu Maeva with fine views of Huahine's mountains, this resort offers a mix of over-water and land-based bungalows and bungalow-like hotel rooms. Beach however is not as sandy as the one at Te Tiare Beach Resort *(see below)*. $$$

Te Tiare Beach Resort, BP 36, Fare, www.tetiarebeach.com, tel: 606050, fax: 606051. Huahine's most luxurious all-bungalow resort has a fine beach, lagoon and views of the nearby islands. Its bungalows are among the largest and best equipped in French Polynesia. Although the resort is on the main island, guests are ferried to and from by boat so that it seems like an offshore resort. $$$

Relais Mahana, BP 30, Fare, Huahine (Avera near Huahine's south end), tel: 688154, fax: 688508, www.relaismahana.pf. This newly renovated hotel sits on the territory's best beach and lagoon. Located on the south end of the island, it is quite isolated. $$

Chez Guynette, BP 87, Fare, tel: 688375, e-mail: chezguynette@mail.pf. Basic hostel-style hotel opposite the town dock with simple rooms, dormitory and a communal kitchen where you can cook your own meals; restaurant and bar open for breakfast and lunch. $

Raiatea and Tahaa

Le Taha'a Private Island & Spa, BP 67, Patio, Tahaa, tel: 698400, fax: 698401, www.letahaa.com. One of French

Polynesia's most luxurious resorts, opened in 2002 on Motu Tautau, 40-minutes by boat from Raiatea airport. Guest bungalows – some with views of Bora Bora–are among the largest here, especially those ashore. $$$

Raiatea Hawaiki Nui Hotel, BP 43, Uturoa, www.pearlresorts.com, tel: 600500, fax: 662020. The world's first over-water bungalows were built here in 1968 at the edge of the reef cliff to compensate for lack of a beach. Renovations have modernized these as well as the hotel-style rooms. The only international-standard hotel on the island. $$$

Sunset Beach Motel, BP 397, Uturoa, www.raiatea.com/sunsetbeach, tel: 663347, fax: 663308. Some 20 self-contained cottages sit in a coconut grove beside a beach with stunning views of Bora Bora on the horizon. No restaurant or other facilities. $$

Bora Bora

Hotel Bora Bora, BP 1, Vaitape, tel: 604411, fax: 604422, www.amanresorts.com. Bora Bora's first major hotel was built in 1961 on Pointe Raititi, at the western end of gorgeous Matira Beach, and upgraded to super-luxury status in the late 1990s by Aman Resorts. Only the thatch-topped main building remains

from the original. New bungalows are exquisitely appointed. This the only Bora Bora resort without a swimming pool, although a few bungalows on land have their own small pools. $$$

Bora Bora Lagoon Resort, BP 175, Vaitape (on Motu Toopua, 1km (½ mile) off Vaitape), tel: 604000, fax: 604001, www.boraboralagoonresort.orient-express.com. On northern end of hilly Motu Toopua, 10 minutes by boat from Vaitape village, this luxury resort sports a thatch-roof main building, large swimming pool, well-appointed bungalows and a spa. Bungalows are positioned close together. $$$

Bora Bora Nui Resort & Spa, BP 502, 98730 Vaitape, tel: 603200, fax: 603201, www.boraboranui.com. On southern end of Motu Toopua, 15 minutes by boat from Vaitape, this new 120-unit St. Regis hotel has some of French Polynesia's largest and most luxurious guest bungalows (with canopy beds and large marble bathrooms), a majority of them over-water. $$$

Bora Bora Pearl Beach Resort, BP 169, Vaitape, tel: 605200, fax: 605222, www.pearlhotels.com. Located on flat Motu Tevairoa, 10-minute boat ride from the main island's northwestern point, this resort has as much Polynesian style as any other Bora Bora hotel. Thatch, bamboo and coconut wood lend island charm to the bungalows, some with private gardens and plunge pools. $$$

Inter-Continental Bora Bora Beachcomber Resort, BP 156, Vaitape, tel: 604900, fax: 604999, www.interconti.com. Now exclusive and nearly on a par with Bora Bora's other top resorts, this former Moana Beach Parkroyal has had a major face-lift to all public areas and over-water bungalows. Excellent beachside location on eastern side of Matira Point. $$$

Le Meridien Bora Bora, BP 190, Vaitape, tel: 605151, fax: 605110, www.lemeridien-tahiti.com. On northern end

---

👁 Over-water bungalows

In 1968, in the absence of a beach, the three young American owners of the Hotel Bali Hai Raiatea – now the Raiatea Hawaiki Nui Hotel – built several guest bungalows out on the reef and connected them to shore by a pier. Such over-water bungalows are now the most popular and expensive type of accommodation in French Polynesia.

With thatch roofs, steps descending into the lagoon from private decks, and glass floor panels through which guests can watch fish swim in the lagoon below, they are the personification of romance.

of Motu Pitiaau, 5 minutes by boat from Anau, this large resort has a fine beach and lagoon, and excellent snorkelling nearby. Most bungalows are over-water but are smaller than other comparable resorts. $$$

Sofitel Marara, BP 6, Nunue, tel: 677046, fax: 677403, www.accorhotels.com. Built in the 1970s to house a movie crew, this all-bungalow resort sits on the eastern portion of Matira Beach, and has a good array of watersports. It plays second ukulele to its sister, the Sofitel Motu *(see below)*. $$$

Sofitel Motu, BP 516, Nunue, tel: 605600, fax: 605666, www.accorhotels.com. On Piti Uuuta islet, 5 minutes from the Sofitel Marara, this more intimate and luxurious alternative has the best views of any Bora Bora resort from its over-water and hillside bungalows. $$$

Bora Bora Beach Resort, BP 943, Vaitape, tel: 605950, fax: 605951, www.polynesian-resort-hotels.com. Opened in 2003 on Matira Beach between Sofitel Marara and Le Maitai Polynesia, this attractive hotel has a better beach but lacks the amenities of its neighbours. Minimally-appointed motel-style rooms sit across the road from restaurant, bar and pool. $$

Club Méditerranée Bora Bora, BP 34, Vaitape, tel: 429699 or 604604, fax: 421683, www.clubmed.com. Fun-filled, all-inclusive resort has both bungalows and hotel rooms. Good value for the sports-minded. $$

Hotel Matira, BP 31, Vaitape, tel: 677051, fax: 677702, www.hotelmatira.com. A collection of Indonesian-style cottages on Matira peninsula. Few services or amenities. $$

Le Maitai Polynesia, BP 505, Vaitape, tel: 603000, fax: 676603, www.hotel-maitai.com. The round-island road runs through this beachside resort aimed at moderate-income travellers. Over-water bungalows are charming but smaller than at other resorts. Most units

are hillside hotel rooms, some with lagoon and Raiatea/ Tahaa views. $$

Rangiroa

Kia Ora Sauvage, BP 4607, Papeete, www.hotelkiaora.com, tel: 960222, fax: 960220. Only 10 Robinson Crusoes allowed at a time at French Polynesia's most remote resort – on a tiny islet one hour by boat from the airport. Five rustic but comfortable guest bungalows have private baths but no electricity. $$$

Kia Ora Village, BP 4607, Papeete, www.hotelkiaora.com, tel: 960222, fax: 960220. Rangiroa's premiere resort was built lagoonside in early 1970s; it now has over-water bungalows as well as beach bungalows with hot tubs. New swimming pool and good selection of watersports and lagoon tours. $$$

Les Relais de Joséphine, BP 140, Ava-toru, tel and fax: 960200, e-mail: relaisjosephine@mail.pf. Comfortable guest house with bungalows. Has no beach but a wonderful view of dolphins at play in Tiputa Pass. Good family-style French meals served at its restaurant. $$

Manihi

Manihi Pearl Beach Resort, BP 2460, Papeete, tel: 431610 or 964273, fax: 431786 or 964272, www.pearlre-sorts.com. Only resort on Manihi has a rocky beach but good swimming pool and watersports facilities. Its over-water and beach bungalows exude an evocative Polynesian style. $$$

Tikihau

Tikihau Pearl Beach Resort, BP 20, Tuherahera, Tikehau, tel: 431610 or 962300, fax: 429914 or 962301, www.pearlresorts.com. Rustic exterior belies its luxurious interiors at Tikihau's only resort. Swimming pool, sand beach and excellent diving nearby. Some over-water bungalows hover over the shallow pass into the lagoon. $$$

Index